TOWARD A COSMIC THEOLOGY

TOWARD A COSMIC THEOLOGY

CHRISTIAN REVELATION IN A VAST UNIVERSE

Thomas F. O'Meara, OP

Paulist Press
New York / Mahwah, NJ

Cover image by NASA images / Shutterstock.com
Cover and book design by Lynn Else

Library of Congress Cataloging-in-Publication Data
Names: O'Meara, Thomas F., 1935– author.
Title: Toward a cosmic theology: Christian revelation in a vast universe / Thomas F. O'Meara, OP.
Description: Paperback. | New York ; Mahwah, NJ : Paulist Press, [2024] | Includes bibliographical references. | Summary: "This book considers the main areas of Christian revelation from new perspectives drawn from astrophysics and science"— Provided by publisher.
Identifiers: LCCN 2023039855 (print) | LCCN 2023039856 (ebook) | ISBN 9780809156863 (paperback) | ISBN 9780809188512 (ebook)
Subjects: LCSH: Religion and science. | Science—Religious aspects—Christianity.
Classification: LCC BL240.3 .O455 2024 (print) | LCC BL240.3 (ebook) | DDC 261.5/5—dc23/eng/20240205
LC record available at https://lccn.loc.gov/2023039855
LC ebook record available at https://lccn.loc.gov/2023039856

ISBN 978-0-8091-5686-3 (paperback)
ISBN 978-0-8091-8851-2 (e-book)

Published by Paulist Press
997 Macarthur Boulevard
Mahwah, New Jersey 07430
www.paulistpress.com

Printed and bound in the
United States of America

We have only to look at the planets and suns.
They will provide us with enough problems to solve.

Johann Wolfgang Goethe

CONTENTS

CONTENTS

INTRODUCTION

A human on Earth—growing crops, climbing a mountain, fashioning a mosaic, or sending radio signals to stars—lives in a vast universe.

On a clear summer night in the Northern Hemisphere, the Andromeda Galaxy can sometimes be seen. This faint blur of light in a dark sky comes from a galaxy that is relatively near to the Earth's own galaxy, the Milky Way. A galaxy has around a hundred to two hundred billion stars and is the building block of a universe of fire and matter, of gravity and light. With a diameter of about 220,000 light-years, Andromeda has many families of suns. Approximately 2.5 million light-years away, it is moving toward the Milky Way at sixty-eight miles a second. The two galaxies are expected to merge in approximately 4.5 billion years.

So many stars. Scientists on Earth learned recently that these suns can have planets. So many planets. So many forms of life. Probably so many intelligent societies. So many worlds.

TWO PERSPECTIVES AND THEIR DIALOGUE

Terrestrial mathematicians and scientists have pondered the universe for centuries. What were its beginnings? Are stars alive? In the late twentieth century, various scholars saw links between ancient societies and the stars. George Coyne, for example, wrote,

> As we look back at our ancestors we realize that one of the first goals of their journey was to see the heavens, their lives, nature, and all that was happening to them as a gift from on high. In fact, the cosmos was a stage on which the human adventure was acted out. There was the sky so clear and yet so dark that one could not help but be moved by admiration and wonder for a beauty worthy of the one who had made it.[1]

The cave paintings from the Paleolithic Age were not just pictures of hunted animals but sometimes outlines of constellations. What was their influence on life on Earth? Thirty thousand years ago, biological, human, and social ages were entwined with a wide, cosmic time. Jo Marchant notes, "Lascaux Cave is as much about cosmology as it is about biology. Rather than copying their immediate surroundings, the artists were synthesizing all of the changes—on the Earth and in the sky—that defined their existence. It was an ode to their universe and represented humanity's first ideas about the nature of the cosmos and the origins of life."[2] The animals that were painted on the walls were those in the sky. Astronomy and faith were linked through the stars, and were interacting with art, science, and religion.

Observations, questions, and deductions coming from the human spirit have led to beliefs about something we define as the Ultimate. What or who plans the size and variety of a "cosmos"? Most people pursue some ideas, emotions, and activities associated with religion. Moreover, those who follow a religion have usually concluded that they have been contacted, albeit silently, by some form of revelation from the divine. Believers and theologians, like scientists, are coming to grasp that we cannot understand the natural world only through past stories and axioms. Stars and their planets can suggest further life-forms in solar civilizations—living beings with different biologies and ecologies. Furthermore, these life-forms imply planetary intelligences with their psychologies, anthropologies, and theologies.

Faith need not be born of fear, guilt, or fantasy; it can be born of awe. Faith can be a quest for knowledge of the unseen: a quest for help, happiness, and life. Religions, contemplating the size and motion of the stars, have often learned from science. Science begins with presuppositions about the reality and order of the physical world; theology begins with human experience of God as mediated by humanity's experience of life. Both are fashioned by some kind of faith.

Science and religion have similarities. They both provide ways of looking at the world and its underlying dynamic. Both the forces at work in nature and personal existence can be revelatory of human creativity or of the Absolute. Science, with its language of atoms and suns in an ever-expanding universe, is important for the believer in something greater. Throughout history, the cosmos has provided humans with religious imagery.

Enlightenment in modern centuries brought disdain toward religion. Science saw Christianity, and other religious perspectives, as anti-intellectual, anti-empirical, and oppressive. Consequently, faith and religion became little more than philosophies with views on the existence of a God or on the interactions of divine activity and human freedom that were either weak or incorrect. In fact, Christianity and most religions are concerned with more than philosophical issues. They are about personal contact with a disclosing and loving God, human spiritual maturity, and existence beyond dying.

Today, rural Semitic images and Greek metaphysics from the past are being set aside through an understanding of galactic process and stellar unfolding. Religions cannot simply repeat static scriptures and dogmas; they may often welcome new facts from science. Religions have their deformities: science can help to identify and counter them and keep people away from superstition, fundamentalism, and neo-paganism. Religion and science are no longer competing. They are not—through apologetics or dismissal—trying to replace each other. Some scientists note the importance of religion to connect people to the universe as it is being discovered. Joseph Bracken, for example, sees a fresh dialogue between religion and science: "Both sides now realize better than ever before that only together can they find practical solutions to significant social issues. Both groups now see better the inevitable limitations of their disciplines."[3] Science and religion are mutual truth seekers.

Today, few people are interested in deriving science or revelation from each other. Scientific cosmology is the study of the universe, past and present, while an adult religious faith looks at humans touched by divine presence. Through research and faith, human beings are trying to make sense of the vast universe that can reflect something of what religions call "God." John Haught writes,

> The anticipatory religious longing for a saving transcendent rightness is perhaps the most adventurous instance of striving in the whole story of life. Religious strivings for communion within a transcendent unity, billions of years of cosmic activity, along with the enormity of space and an emerging physical complexity receive a new narrative coherence.[4]

Together, science and faith can contribute a richer view of reality than either can achieve on its own. This new maturity in faith and the perspectives of science have come together.

Religious faith and natural science are two paths in this dynamic of convergence. They arrive at a synthesis in which both science and faith keep their own identities even as they relate closely to each other as they express their own realms of truth.[5]

Tonight, as on every night, powerful instruments of research receiving radio and light waves search out stars far away. However, they are examining stars in a new way. They are looking for planets circling around those stars. Since 1992, more than six thousand "exoplanets" outside of our solar system have been detected. More instruments gathering light are being constructed and launched to search for civilizations and cultures on planets, in our galaxy and beyond. Astronomers note that planets resembling Earth are not rare and so some are likely to have intelligent life. William Stoeger observed that although "we as yet have no direct knowledge of biology anywhere else, we can surmise that whatever life has emerged elsewhere, it must be based on the same principles of physics and chemistry. But that leaves open an enormous number of possibilities."[6] Science is expanding the possibility of varied cultural contacts.

ASTROTHEOLOGY

In these pages, astrotheology considers the structures of the universe—past, present, and future—to illumine faith, and specifically, Christian faith. Ideas and thought forms for theologies are drawn from contemporary astrophysics and cosmology. For Lutheran theologian Ted Peters, it is "that branch of theology which provides a critical analysis of the contemporary space sciences combined with an explication of classic doctrines such as creation and Christology for the purpose of constructing a comprehensive and meaningful understanding of our human situation within an astonishingly immense cosmos."[7] Scientists' understanding of the structures of the universe has developed considerably throughout the last two centuries, and in the last fifty years the general public has gained a greater awareness of astronomy and cosmology as new, powerful telescopes are launched. In recent decades, theologians have looked at the intersections of Christian theology with phenomena being discovered in the universe. Science can expand and enrich Earth's understanding of God and his activities and plans, while faith can encourage the scientist to expect numerous but organized projects. Contemporary sciences point to what the Ultimate has planned for Earth and its evolving cosmos. Both search into the future: faith's revelation expects a positive future; while science studies a universe that has order, beauty, and life.

What Christianity calls "salvation history" can have modalities on other worlds. On Earth, it encompasses histories, while believing hope views it as ending in the transformations of living beings. Religion contemplates aspects of a world with a lengthy past and a long future coming to be. Haught begins his view of astrotheology with cosmic history. There can be histories of God's love on other planets:

> The epic of the universe is no less a story about emerging subjectivity than about the movement of atoms, molecules, cells, and social groups. With the relatively recent arrival of distinctly religious experience in cosmic history and with the ever-expanding knowledge of the size of the realms of stars, the universe reaches out toward horizons previously unknown.[8]

Other planets with their own geologies and solar systems might have their own beliefs and realities of faith.

Cosmic theology sees galactic clusters in their development and variety, in their promise and goal. God is beyond being a judge and emerges as the architect of destinies for areas of the cosmos. The interpretation of the New Testament's message can be advanced by the natural sciences. Faiths can be illuminated by bosons and star clusters. For astrotheology divine love and empowerment are widely present atmospheres. Faith, far from establishing a small devotional sect, urges all to discard smallness and to venture forth into the uncharted ocean of civilizations. Coyne observes that new ideas about unfolding areas in the birth and death of stars give "new insights into classical theological themes, such as the human body and soul, freedom, sin and redemption; death and resurrection."[9] On twin planets or at a subatomic intersection of particles, there is the sacramental, the mystical, the revelatory. David Toolan sees cosmology as theological:

> God's energy, glory, favor, and promise should be seen shining throughout the whole of things, not just at the beginning but throughout all time and history, coming like the background radiation of the Big Bang from everywhere at once and with the same resonating intensity, a rampant, quickening energy that is the presence of the Holy Spirit immanent in the material world.[10]

Whether it be on the distinct worlds of an expanding galaxy or in a particle's merger, there can be many modes of God's presence. Religion is not about miracles or visions but about the Trinity in the cosmic. The Source of all has written a tremendous symphony whose melodies the stars, galaxies, and planets play.[11]

The following chapters are not science and not a philosophy of religion. They offer questions for and insights into Christian revelation and faith by looking at structures of nature, large and small. These pages spend no time proving anything in religious faith from scientific observations. Millennia ago, words born of an intersection of Hebrew and Greek thinking expressed an enterprise that was called contemplating Wisdom. Wisdom knows the disposition of the whole world, and the powers in the elements, the beginning and the ending, and the midst of the times. In the Bible, Wisdom's direction and initiative assist God in beginning and fashioning the universe. Wisdom knows the seasons of the year and the dispositions of the stars (cf. Wis 7:17–19).

Is today a further Genesis? The French scientist and theologian, Jacques Arnould, sees the new paths of science as beginnings: "These reflective experiences offer the occasion to look in new ways at Christian tradition. They will give an importance to other quite different beings. They will set forth in a new light important aspects of faith. They will illumine areas unimagined."[12] On Earth, exploration and science join with hope and confident faith to enter the drama of the universe: "The sky is opening up to us, but at the price of a revolution in thought."[13]

PART I
THE UNIVERSE
Dynamics and Sources

1

IN A VAST UNIVERSE

For humans, reality ranges from a solar eclipse to an individual bee just hatched. Enormous planets, minute particles, red suns, blue gasses, and dark matter are just a few of the beings in a totality, a vast universe. Scientists are seeking to understand the forces unfolding over billions of years. That ensemble of fire and matter, light and gas continues to move farther out into the space it fashions, at forty miles a second in all directions. A universe.

Around three thousand stars in the Milky Way are visible to human eyes on clear nights. Earth's galaxy holds more than two hundred billion suns—so many stars above and around one planet with one sun and one moon. Even using a greatly improved level of technology it would take fifty to eighty thousand years for a human being to travel to the nearest star. To reach another galaxy, it would take 750 million years. To get to the limit of the known universe would take humans 225 trillion years. Experts consider the exact size of the universe to be unknown but estimate it at 93 trillion light-years in diameter. That area with its countless galaxies is constantly growing. A vast universe.

THE BIG BANG

In the 1960s, there occurred a detection of radio waves reaching in all directions from Earth and its solar system. They suggested that there had been an initial explosion of the universe in the distant past. Thirteen and a half billion years ago that beginning brought forth a small but dense reality—a ball of heat in which future forms of matter and energy were seminally present. In terms of time and space that primal event occurred everywhere at once. There was nothing before it. Brian Greene explains, "The Big Bang did not take place at one point; instead, the Big Bang eruption took place *everywhere* in an infinite expanse."[1]

In the fractions of the first seconds, some thirteen billion years ago, all the material in the universe today was created in a dense fireball. A trillionth of a second later, the universe was filled with extraordinarily hot and dense planes of energy; their temperature was a billion times hotter than the core of the sun today. After further seconds, subatomic particles were binding together to form protons and neutrons: the building blocks of matter and the elements to come.[2] What follows the explosion was distinction, separation between objects, and evolution producing arrays of beings. In that explosion of energy in all directions, scientists find a remarkable consonance of forces that directs many of its dynamics and objects.[3] After two hundred million years, stars had formed, and after four hundred million years, there were galaxies of stars. One specific sun was formed around four billion years later, and its planet Earth has been in place for the past 4.5 billion years. As Joseph Bracken notes,

> The most pivotal moments in the evolution of the universe are those in which balance and order suddenly change, yielding cosmic arenas qualitatively

different from those of preceding eras. Current theory holds that the universe went through a number of these transitions in its earliest moments. Furthermore there is an even grander sense, a meta-sense in which symmetry lies at the core of an evolving cosmos.[4]

Today, telescopes can see back in time to how the universe looked when protogalaxies were being formed. When a galaxy near the edge of the cosmos appears in a telescope, observers on Earth see it as it appeared more than several billion years ago.

Astronomers estimate that, during the past ten billion years, the universe has expanded in each direction by a factor of three. Everything—individuals and suns—is rushing way from everything else; there are increasing separations between galaxies, each with its hundreds of millions of stars. Scientists see seventy-two kilometers a second as one measurement of the speed of this expansion. The explosion of all the galaxies is complicated by the movement of the beings of the universe in various directions.

In the cosmos, light is the cosmic connector, the subatomic enabler, the galactic arranger. Science tells us that long ago light exploded into all that would be reality. Everything is penetrated by light. Nicolas Cheetham writes,

> Tonight the light of an ancient supernova will finally reach Earth....For millions of years, this luminous conflagration has surged across the universe, carried on a wave of photons traveling at 300,000 kilometers per second (186,000 miles per second). Century by century, decade by decade, year by year, it has relentlessly plowed towards us....Traveling 5.9 million miles a year, there is no swifter messenger for vital information, but the immense scale of

the universe dwarfs even light's velocity, imposing a communication lag between all cosmic events and ourselves. By the time the light of an extragalactic supernova reaches us, entire stellar generations will have passed away in their home galaxy.[5]

Light's universal presence is a kind of natural cosmic grace or sacrament.

Amid all the realities in the universe there is still the surprising conclusion, first, that "the universe is largely empty."[6] The countless stars in the cosmos are occupying only 4 percent of the volume of space in the universe at present. Interspersed among clusters of stars or groups of galaxies are immense fields of emptiness where very few burning suns are to be found. Much of the universe, remarkably cold, is a great quasi-void into which what exists, or will exist, moves.

Second, there is a discrepancy between two realities: the amount of visible matter and the strength of gravity in the universe coming from that matter. This has led to the postulation of a further kind of matter: "dark matter." This unusual material, yet to be empirically detected, is dark because it seemingly is not made of anything that radiates, reflects, or absorbs light. Dark matter is invisible not because it is unlit but because it does not interact with light. It does not emit light as stars do; it does not reflect light as happens with planets, moons, and clouds of gas. It does not emit or absorb x-rays, radio waves, or any form of radiation that scientists have so far detected. "Dark" here is not sinister; it does not deform or obscure. Around each galaxy there seems to be an atmosphere of dark particles surrounding the visible stars and gas. They far outweigh all that is visible as they contribute a huge amount of mass to the universe. Most of the matter holding the Milky Way and other galaxies together seems to be this dark matter not easily perceived. Only 4 percent of the universe is made up of the beings and forms of matter with which we are familiar. Around 24 percent is invisible dark matter. Seventy-two percent is something further: "dark energy." Dark energy signifies whatever is causing the universe to move outward and apart. Little progress has been made in finding out much about it. A force in empty space makes the universe expand in many directions; something is pushing the universe apart.

GALAXIES AND THE MILKY WAY

The many galaxies in the universe are the nations of the stellar world. A galaxy is a *gravitationally* bound system of *stars*, *gas*, *dust*, and *dark matter*; many of them came and went billions of years ago; many will coalesce far in the future. A galaxy comprises star clusters and solar systems—and their planets. The number of stars in a galaxy varies, but astronomers assume that there are around one hundred to two hundred and fifty billion stars per galaxy. There are different kinds of galactic formations from ellipse to spiral. Today, the number of galaxies in the universe is estimated at around two hundred billion.

Clusters and galaxies are families of stars—stars of different sizes, colors, life cycles, and various orbiting speeds. The sun with planet Earth in its gravitational field is moving within a collection of one to two hundred billion stars called for some time and in various linguistic versions "the Milky Way." Earth's location is in a spiral arm of the galaxy, one of four flowing out from a core. At the center of this galaxy is a supermassive black hole. Caleb Scharf concludes,

> We are living in a relatively unexceptional part of the Milky Way. Within fifty light-years of us are some 130 stars that are visible at night to the naked eye, and at least ten times more stars that are detectable

with telescopes. That is not much....Still our species at present has no way of crossing to even the closest stellar neighbor in less that about 40,000 years. In that sense we are an island in the interstellar worlds.[7]

Other galaxies along with the Milky Way, Andromeda, and the two Magellan clouds visible in the Southern Hemisphere form a "local group." This cluster of galaxies (more than fifty members) belongs to a larger cluster called the Virgo Cluster, whose center is fifty-three million light years away and holds fifteen hundred to two thousand galaxies. Recent research indicates that this supercluster is a "lobe" of an even greater cluster: it has been given the name Laniakea, a Hawaiian word for "immense heaven." This supercluster is drawing galaxies to its center in great numbers—one hundred thousand of them. The cosmos is enormous.

STAR CREATURES

Stars bring planets. Matter and gas produce a small ball that orbits one of the new stars, a celestial object becoming a planet. Robert O'Dell writes, "All of the stars there [in the constellation of Orion within the Milky Way] have associated circumstellar disks, which means that all of them have the building blocks of planets. What goes on in those stars is probably what has gone on in most other stars."[8] Beginning in 1992, planets outside our solar system were detected, celestial objects now called "exoplanets." Today, there is an extensive search for exoplanets. In less than thirty years, over six thousand planets have been discovered beyond our solar system, and new telescopes have been launched to search out possible planets. One planet has been found in another galaxy. Estimates project the number of planets, just in the Milky Way, to be possibly several billion. With them, Earth has entered a new kind of universe.

The great number of stars suggests that many suns have planets, some with life-forms, and perhaps not a few with intelligent cultures. In our galaxy, a number of these planets resemble Earth, and some circle their stars in "a habitable zone," that is, a zone conducive to life. Finding a planet in a habitable zone around a star, like our sun, is a significant step toward finding planets like Earth. Planets resembling Earth and so capable of having intelligent life are not rare. Chet Raymo notes how the knowing and free inhabitants of other planets might have their astrophysical periods and historical ages: "A hundred generations of stars lived and died in the Milky Way galaxy before the sun was born. There were generations of stars turning hydrogen into the stuff of future planets."[9] Even lengthy histories come to an end. Meanwhile, new planets are on their way toward fashioning their own sciences, arts, and religions.

Human beings are part of the universe. All things, living and inanimate, receive their elements from solar and galactic processes. Whatever is on a planet emerges there not only from water and lava but from the minerals born of stellar explosions. Earth and other planets are composed of complex atoms that were created inside ancient stars or during stellar supernovas and then flung out to travel through space. The iron in human blood comes from the iron in stars that were new hundreds of millions of years ago. The brains and animating principles of intelligent beings are made up of minute particles from star's atoms. Each human is composed of waves and particles with a lengthy past. Scientists reflect, "Send your consciousness backwards through time at lightning speed, past your parents and grandparents, through your primate ancestors and down through all the animals that preceded them."[10] Each person is a collective permeated by a history. Thomas Aquinas wrote that the human person was a summary of aspects of the spectrum of being: "Although they are dispersed throughout creation, these many realities of goodness are brought together in the human being. The person is like the horizon, the intersection, and the edge where corporeal nature and spiritual nature meet."[11] Stars, planets, and persons inhabit a universe still emerging from the Big Bang. George Coyne observed,

> We are constantly exchanging atoms with the total reservoir of atoms in the universe, as each year ninety-eight percent of the atoms in our bodies are renewed. Each time we breathe we take in billions and billions of neutrinos recycled by the rest of breathing organisms during recent weeks. Nothing in my genes was present a year ago. It is all new, regenerated from the available energy and matter in the universe.[12]

The world implies and discloses a little of the plans of the intelligent Source of a universe. One astronomer finds "an intricate network of regularities, constraints, and relationships which actually operate, linking everything with everything else but also constituting each entity's individuality and relative independence."[13] The divine seems to be far beyond the thin definitions of Earth's philosophies and religions.

COUNTLESS BEINGS IN THE COSMOS

Beings are planned, loved, and empowered into existence. So, why does the Eternal create? Thomas Aquinas wrote, "The beings of nature are produced by divine art. In a sense they are works of art coming from God himself. Every artisan intends for his work the best over-all situation; not in an absolute sense but in terms of its particular goal."[14] Jacques Arnould concludes,

In its fascinating variety the world shows the fact that relatively simple physical elements can organize themselves into systems of astonishing complexity....It shows that the physics of our universe is fashioned to make development to the highest degree possible is astonishing, almost unbelievable. This is a much greater miracle then occasional interventions of a supernatural designer.[15]

John Haught notes the ancient Greek verbal insight that the universe is a "cosmos," something beautiful. Stellar phenomena are visually striking. "As we explore the universe we should ask not only about the meaning of intelligence but also about what the existence of beauty implies for the essential character [of] the whole universe....Perhaps the aim toward beauty is enough to endow the universe with purpose."[16]

Astrophysics expands the human understanding of the breadth of the universe, while faith accepts the reality of deeper, invisible modalities of divine presence and revelation. Faith affirms further divine gifts and modes of presence— shares in degrees of divine life. Other planets with their civilizations could receive their own special inspirations from divine life. They too have "reigns of God" as atmospheres bring deeper life, unusual changes, and transformations for individuals and societies.[17]

Throughout billions of years, galaxies give birth to solar systems and planets. There are parts of the universe where stars are not visible even to powerful telescopes. It is likely that civilizations on some of them will have concrete projects in art, science, religion, and technology. The theologian Heidi Russell suggests,

What might we learn from these cosmic observations about our own small but not insignificant, part in the human and cosmic story? We might learn to value the complexity that comes from a system having a large number of parts as a reflection of the beauty of God's creation....We can embrace the fractal beauty that comes out of the complexity of human life lived on the edge of chaos.[18]

Science and faith urge people to approach beauty, to see a vast universe, and to expect an extensive future.

2

ORIGIN, GUIDE, AND DESTINY

The universe points to a beginning, to structural evolutions, and to plans. It points to a Mind, a Source.

Christianity, like most religions on Earth, teaches that the universe has been created by an ultimate Reality called "God," in English. Thomas Aquinas warned that knowledge pointing toward an Absolute can only indicate mainly what the divine is not. God remains eminently unknown.[1] Religious thinkers, however, presume that their sacred books describe a divinity, although insightful theologians and mystics hold that finite knowledge can grasp very little concerning an infinite Cause. Rational arguments for the existence of a deity are, at most, intimations drawn from the physical world directed toward the existence of something greater. Is God a distant watcher? A cold judge?

Research into the cosmos continues to find new realities and patterns. The size of galaxies, small and gigantic planets, and particles existing for a fraction of a second make up a remarkable diversity. Their realities and forces suggest new ways of thinking about the divine. Scientific information about the breadth and complexity of the universe can assist in considering the reality of a God. Theology may learn about divine projects from astrophysics: it fashions a spirituality of anticipation and a belief in transformation and sets aside the atmosphere of laws and devotions.[2] God is a statement and a question.

WHAT IS "GOD"?

Early in the Middle Ages, Alanus de Insulis wrote that God is "an infinite sphere the center of which is everywhere and the circumference is nowhere."[3] A century later, Thomas Aquinas saw God as "an infinite and indeterminate sea of reality."[4] Throughout the centuries, the word "God"—*Deus, theos, elohim, Allah, Gott, Dio*—has had scientific, philosophical, and religious meanings. It often implied some anthropomorphic image, and the word took on political ideas associated with "lord," "king," "queen," and "priest." In hundreds of languages, the word "God" can mean one supreme being or it may mean beings that are divine auxiliaries.

Thinkers writing in Greek or Latin pondered a Supreme Being while modern German philosophers systematized an Absolute becoming itself in history. Traditional words and definitions like "all-knowing," infinite," "ubiquitous," while not false, are limited. Some scientists imply that any god would be incomplete, withdrawn, detached; others hold that a deity cannot know the future, does not influence beings, and may be weak or even hostile. In recent centuries, many of the questions raised by science about religion, however, are what philosophy and theology have traditionally called "theodicy." They feature issues of logic and metaphysics, and spotlight conundrums about a supreme deity and its links to finite beings. They are concerned with philosophy and not with religion.

The languages on Earth are many. How numerous might languages be in the universe? And what kinds of languages? Symbols, sounds, pictograms? While each language has its limitations, each has its capabilities to cast light on the realms of being. Languages, and their accompanying theologies, on unusual planets, as they refer to God, might be more mature, more concrete than those on Earth.

DIVINE PLANS

Theologians in the recent century have gone beyond the widespread religious model of a pyramid made of levels of beings with a deity at the top. God is much more than a supreme figure with lofty attributes. Theologies of a godly God could be aided by what astrophysicists uncover. Distances and galactic arrays suggest a new understanding of transcendence while subatomic forces throw light on immanence and inspiration.

To know more about cosmic structures is to learn more about God in his plans and their realizations. Thomas Aquinas wrote that "beings which have intellect have a more complete kind of life in that their self-movement is more complete.... That Being, then, whose nature is its very act of knowledge is the Being which has life in the highest degree. Such a Being is God."[5] The divine mind is the seminal background from which patterns and structures in the universe emerge over billions of years. "God is a living fountain, a fountain not diminished in spite of its continuous flow outwards."[6] The staggering number of stars and animals are in the divine being as string quartets were in Beethoven's imagination. "Divine wisdom contains the seminal ideas of all things, exemplary forms existing in the divine intelligence."[7] Religion is not a playground for miracles but a deeper appreciation of God as a theoretician and a giver. "Even before contingent beings come into existence God sees them as they actually exist; his eternity includes contact in a present moment with the whole of time."[8] Werner Eizinger writes of a primal Source: "The Godly is the Originating. From it and through it the cosmos unfolds. This God is in itself a fullness containing variously everything, both eternity and its unfolding."[9] God is not an individual thing adorned with adjectives like *mysterious* and *infinite* but a radically different reality, intelligible, slightly accessible, and welcoming.

TOWARD A GODLY GOD

Far from being a Byzantine hierarch or a German Kaiser, God is something that sets in motion thousands of clusters of suns with millions of planets, and through them all sorts of worlds that hold both black holes and birds. Intelligent beings on distant and unusual planets might understand the Ultimate in different and more explicit ways.

Christian theology affirms God to be more than a creator. Beyond divine attributes like existence and goodness there is special religious information, revelation about and personal contact with God. Faith affirms a Person who, in silence, really contacts men and women at deeper levels. Religions profess special "supernatural" presences like "salvation," "redemption," "predestination," "charismatic inspiration" beyond or within the networks of being. Jesus spoke of an atmosphere of "abundant life" (John 10:10). These modes of life rooted not in gravity and fire but in divine presence offer further gifts to knowing creatures: a "participation," a "share," a "communion," a "fulfillment." Aquinas affirmed of this higher life for intelligent beings: "God alone makes people godlike by communicating a share in his divine nature."[10] Christian theology is moving away from a theodicy of acts to a theology of life, from judgment to presence. Astrophysical information about the enormous size of the universe or the probability of extraterrestrials can lead faith to new implications about the life of the divine.

One can respect the traditional insight that God's eternity is a moment, a now that is quite atemporal. That God is beyond cosmic cycles of birth and death seems obvious, and yet the Christian belief in a Trinity on mission to Earth and an incarnation in one human being suggests some slight facet of alteration in the divine fullness. Karl Rahner wrote,

> It remains inevitably true that the Logos became man, that the changing history of this human reality is his own history. Thus our time became the time of the eternal, our death is a death involving the immortal God himself....He who is unchangeable in himself can himself become something, he who is unchangeable in himself can himself become subject to change in something else.[11]

God can enter time in ways that he chooses; the Bible states that God's special love does occur in history. The grace of God no longer comes down from on high, from a God transcending the world and without history; it is in the cosmos in tangible historical forms even as they are very minor aspects of the divine realm. Galactic newness and alteration exist along with the sovereign otherness of the divine being.

When billions of beings emerge out of mental plans into the richness of their own being and life for the first time, those realities of what was once only potential should have some effect.

A CAUSAL WORLD

Given this vast universe—how does God act in this world? Does the force beginning the Big Bang continue to influence a diversely expanding universe? Does it only plan a few explosions for long ago? Is it involved in producing planets with their own ecologies and literatures two billion years from now? Does it contact the inner life of intelligent beings in realms of religion on planets that will flourish in the future?

Aquinas singled out being-a-cause as an important endowment of reality. God is not the only cause in the universe, and beings are not merely fleeting phenomena at its disposal. There is only one ultimate or "primary cause," God. This original cause remains involved with everything. Other beings, wherever they might be, are "secondary causes." They are not marionettes; they are real agents acting out of their species' forms to fashion being and life. Newly born gorillas are directly and formally caused by their parents, while indirectly bananas, sunlight, and oxygen contribute to their growth. The causal reality of every being is a power, a gift, a dignity. "On account of the abundance of his goodness (and not at all as a defect in power) God communicates to creatures the dignity of causality."[12] The universe unfolds from and through the effects of these proper, proximate causes. Thus, the activity of God is not the immediate, main, proximate cause of most things. Through the mediation of suitably adapted causes, "the divine will prearranges a mode for things from the formats of its wisdom."[13] The causalities of creatures can be the executors of divine plans, and beings acting out of their natures do not detract from what is the sole, primary cause of all. The medieval professor observed that the ultimate causality is so powerful and complex that it can permit creatures to act in their own ways. It is not out of God's incompleteness or weakness that causal power is given to creatures but out of a fullness of reality and power capable of sharing itself with all. To ignore the distinction between primary and secondary causes is to replace God by a creature or to replace the creature by God. "It is clear that a single effect is not attributed to its natural cause and to God as if one part was from God and the other from the natural agent: it is totally from both but differently."[14] The beings of the universe have varying modes of power and life.

"The divine will is a most powerful agent, but its effects are caused in all kinds of ways according to the arrangement of its wisdom...with the mediation of other causes."[15]

Theologians write of the importance of considering causality given the new directions in matter emerging in scientific fields. William Stoeger, for example, wrote of the importance of considering causality as a dynamic like those in the cosmos:

> Over the past century there has been an explosion of knowledge and understanding about all aspects of nature and of the vast universe of which we are a part. Along with the emerging details of physics, chemistry, biochemistry, and biology from focused scientific research has come a more refined awareness of the many different intricately related factors, "causes," that are at work in nature and in the universe.[16]

Whether from enormous or minute beings, there is an awareness of forces and relationships. Theology has moved from describing God as a *governor* to seeing the divine as *presence*. The myth of an original perfection that is then blocked by a fallen history has been replaced by a cosmic history that is positive, expansive, and transformative. God's activity is both outside and inside the universe, operating as an enabling, creative guide of networks of beings. "God achieves the divine purposes through the undirected unfolding of the potentialities built into the initial framework of creation. This view is 'evolutionary' in that it regards divine guidance as working in and through the normal operations of nature rather than requiring supernatural interventions."[17] The processes of evolution hold their own intrinsic and lengthy dynamics. They do not need external forces to direct or sustain them. They produce great, organized complexity, an unimaginable proliferation of forms of life, and probably varied forms of intelligence. God's power is empowering.

DISCLOSURES OF THE DIVINE

Expansion within galaxies, solar systems, and planets leads to an enormous number of beings and forces in the cosmos. John Haught writes,

> Theology is being challenged in a fresh way today to think about the biblical God in terms of a universe that is largely "self-organizing." What kind of Maker would create a universe in which novelty and creativity emerge mostly at the edge of chaos.[18]

Astrophysics at every turn discloses and explores a universe that is enormous. The new telescopes in space and on mountain ranges will open wider horizons of galaxies. In every way, vast distances and vast arrays continue to unfold. The world is always becoming *more*.

The first and dominant lesson for religion and theology is the depth and breadth of the Divine Reality, an infinity intimated—indeed, displayed—by the size of the universe with its enormous dimensions in light and matter. The general estimate of the size of the universe begins with a diameter of 92 billion light years. Some research now indicates that its size might be significantly larger than that. An expanding universe moves outward; recently, this has been thought to be faster than expected, and perhaps galaxies are moving away from one another with accelerating speeds. The realms of creation include not only worlds now existing although spatially out of sight of Earth but also future stellar assemblies. Who is the Divine Reality behind not just Earth but a myriad of worlds?

Experience of this or that exoplanet could give aspects of its Source. Future sciences, future worlds await.

ONE GOD AND ITS ASSISTANTS

God is not a static deity nor an available coworker for creatures. Early Christian theologians, building upon Jewish traditions and Greek philosophies, faced neighboring religions for whom semidivine agents were important. There were Greek gods and goddesses, Gnostic demiurges, and Semitic angels; they worked under a supreme deity to fashion stars and influence men and women. For instance, Basilides, leader of a school of Christian Gnosticism and teaching in Alexandria in the early second century, was criticized by the theologians Hippolytus of Rome and Irenaeus of Lyons for arranging 365 spheres and forces in the production of the universe. Those agents, forces, and realms were led by semidivine directors.

Today the size of the universe and the intricacy of its areas might suggest some kind of assisting supervisors for cosmic clusters and realms. The size of galactic groups and the number of likely exoplanets could imply auxiliaries sent to regions by the one God. Millions of worlds—one quite different from the other—can suggest that the one ultimate reality delegates responsibility to lesser, pluriform, powerful assistants. Are huge galaxies—clusters of stars with their moons and planets—guided only by the Ultimate? Or are they guided also by intermediate beings? For countless suns and planets there may be powerful beings directing religions and cultures. Through impulses from the one God, they would direct living beings, subtly influence cultures and technologies, and bring revelation and grace to intelligent beings. These vicars are far less, infinitely less, than the fully divine persons of the Trinity but far more than planetary residents. The world or worlds entrusted to each are, nonetheless, a minute area of the universe. Still, beneath and within the cosmos, coming out of the past and the future, is a single Ultimate.

The universe speaks of God. What must this originating imagination be like? Creative vitality seems to be a prominent characteristic of God. Divine life plans and leads forth other living realities. Then it invites those who know and love to share in further life coming from the Source and Destiny. An ancient Christian hymn from the seventh century offers caring and nurturing Latin words: *Alme Conditor siderum*, "You who fashion the stars, you who care for them with love."

3

CLUSTERS, GALAXIES, AND DIVINE TRINITY

Every second, the universe is expanding in all directions by around seventy-five to ninety kilometers per second. Hundreds of thousands of galaxies are moving outward away from Earth.

A COSMOS FILLED WITH GROUPS

Almost all stars (with their planets and moons) are in galaxies: the universe is an assembly of galaxies.[1] Their number is estimated to be around two trillion. The average galaxy holds one hundred to two hundred billion stars. Structures from a single solar system to a galactic supercluster indicate that the basic composition of the universe exists in groups. A dynamic of gathering and clustering reaches through the cosmos.

Stars rarely exist alone. Stars are almost always found in assemblies, in galaxies, in clusters of stars. There is a prominence of groups as gravity draws stars together. Clusters may hold between one hundred thousand and four hundred thousand fiery suns. There are about 150 large groups of stars in the Milky Way. Stars in stages of birth, evolution, merger, and maturity are drawn together through forces not yet fully known. Astronomers speak of "accretion" as one of the most fundamental processes in the universe. As Arwen Rimmer notes, "Triggered by gravity, accretion is the process by which bits of matter accumulate and coalesce with more bits of matter. It works inexorably on all scales to attract and affix smaller things to bigger things....Accretion creates everything there is: galaxies, stars, planets, and eventually, us."[2] Stars seek out other stars.

GOD AS THREE AND ONE

According to Christian revelation, the depth of the one God holds a plurality. A triad emerges from an ontological, mutual communication innate to the divine reality. *Processions*, *nature*, *persons*, *relations*, and *missions* are traditional words that describe this reality. Three self-productive points ("persons" in the language of past Greek culture and metaphysics) enact the Infinite. What Christian theology came to call "persons" in God—Parent, Word, Spirit—are constituted by activities. These three omnipotent centers of activity— knowing, loving, and realizing—emerge in a communion. This makes up, constitutes, or fashions the eternal Divine. Thomas Aquinas saw God not as a supreme being but as a limitless actualization of reality in a realm of life where three activities are distinct eternal persons.[3]

This revelation of three divine activities within knowing and loving brought about a revolution in the image and concept of God.

Christian theologies, however, East and West, have oscillated between an emphasis on one God and a contemplation of three divine realities. Greek and Syriac theologies focused on Father, Son, and Spirit unfolding the divinity,[4] while after the third century, influenced by the political and military organization of the Roman Empire, Western Christianity gave prominence to the one, transcendent God. That supported a tendency to begin and end faith and theology with the one God and to identify the one God with the first person, "Father." From the medieval to the modern era, the one God is dominant in European philosophies and theologies. For instance, Meister Eckhart in the fourteenth century placed the persons of the Trinity on the surface of God, while beneath them is a more inaccessible godhead.

After 1800, modern systems focused on history and process in God. This process occurs in human consciousness, nature and cosmology, the arts, and the history of religions. The three divine powers become themselves. History is a theogony: God is becoming God. The culture and thinking of romantic idealism expressed a trinitarian development present and unfolding in deity, creation, and humanity. History is a progressive, gradually self-disclosing revelation of the Absolute.[5] With the three persons, a world opens: the world of the divine and then of the universe. Marc Maeschalk links this to contemporary thinking.[6] This idealist process, however, seemed to compromise two things: an originally full divinity of God, and the eternal identity of the persons. In the primal godhead, the three persons are incomplete, and in human history, they too are subject to time and change.[7]

In the last century, Christian theologies have been escaping from presuming that God is an emperor, Roman or Baroque. Theologies of the Trinity influenced by time and history unfolding show an interest in relating being and community to each other.[8] While God is necessarily plural and communal, the persons are not separate beings or gods. Leonardo Boff sums up:

> God is Father, Son, and Holy Spirit in reciprocal communion. They coexist from all eternity; none is

before or after the others; none is superior or inferior to the others. Each person enwraps the others; all permeate one another and live in one another. This is the reality of Trinitarian communion. In the beginning there is not the solitude of a timeless One, an eternal being, alone. Rather in the beginning there is the communion of the three unique Ones."[9]

The Trinity is a triunity of activities.

In today's quantum physics, realities in process, events, and temporalities find new situations and relationships. Heidi Russell seeks to illumine the early Greek trinitarian theology of perichoresis—the persons dwelling within each other as well as in themselves—by drawing from "loop quantum gravity" in physics.[10] In this theory, the core of active reality mirrors somewhat the life of the God who created that reality. The three divine forces are the result of each other's dynamism, separate but born of the others. Apparently, both astrophysics and theology are about entities existing and living in fields of activity and creating their worlds.

BEING AS COMMUNAL

The Trinity is not an optional expression of the one deity. This church dogma is not a curious religious linguistic and logical puzzle. That God is somehow pluriform is not asserted as one possible mode of deity. For God, plurality is the necessary mode of being; God exists only as triune. Apparently, the being that is divine can only be communal; it can only be triune. The activity of God vis-à-vis creation is triune not because God (curiously) emerges as three divine persons (like a family) who have decided to work together on projects in the universe (creation, redemption, sanctification). The Trinity is the way God exists, the way God must be. Does being itself—and do realms of beings, stars, and particles—usually hold within their reality a format of community? The universe is constituted not by solitary entities existing in great distances from one another but by dynamic realities in groups. Theologians consider ways in which beings unfold in community. Gisbert Greshake writes, "Creation is determined through relationality and complementarity, plurality and communality."[11]

As a future chapter will consider, minute entities of reality, subatomic particles, flow from fields. Being in its smallest and briefest forms holds its own dynamics and formats of intersubjectivity. Force fields empower a cosmos of tiny subsocieties.[12] Both the Trinity and subatomic particles constitute the world even as each possesses an independence of one another.

Joseph Bracken locates the new conversation between science and religion in a perspective that relates God to the cosmos through universal intersubjectivity born of interactions. God is community in action. Fields of beings result from divine plans and decisions. The "reign of God on Earth" is a special dynamic, a field assisting human beings in mercy and compassion, hope, and service. That mode of living reaches through death into a further world of transformation and amazing life.[13] As Bracken notes,

> Each of the divine persons is a personally ordered society of actual entities and presides over a field of activity proper to its own existence and activity. Three fields of divine activity are fully integrated into a collective field of activity proper to themselves as one God, a divine communion. The activity of the Trinity vis-à-vis the world of creation is always threefold or triune, not because the divine persons have freely decided to work together on the project of creation, redemption, and sanctification

of the world of creation, but because otherwise they could not be one God.[14]

Within a field of unfolding activity caused by the three divine persons, the world of creation has slowly taken shape beginning with the Big Bang. This Christian theology, stimulated by process thinking past and present, sketches an evolving physical universe where the existence and activity of all draws from the energy and resources proper to the divine persons in their ongoing collective field. This reaches from the eternity of God to future eternities with galaxies of a vast variety of creatures. Its processes achieve socially organized realizations in the temporalities of the cosmos that have been set in motion. Russell concludes, "God/Love, who is relation, creates a world that is also relation. Space and time, rather than being the framework of reality, emerge from those relationships that constitute reality. Human beings are not objects or even subjects but rather stories."[15] The dynamic fields reach from the divine being to the quantum physics of fashioning particles.

THE TRIUNE GOD AND OTHER WORLDS

How is the Trinity present to civilizations on other planets? Are its activities in distant and diverse worlds different from those on Earth? Does it reveal to them further aspects of the depths of the divine? On some planets, God may relate to beings mainly as a single primal reality, while on others, the divine may enter their cultures and religions primarily as a triune presence, something more clearly reveled.

Contrary to what religions often assert, contact between God and intelligent creatures is not a mechanics of mental or liturgical activities, not an exchange of rewards for rituals. Intelligent and loving beings are led by God to form societies.

Divine inspirations do not interfere with the dynamics of evolution in the cosmos or with the freedom of intelligent beings: galaxies are in families; stars are in clusters; persons are in societies. God is triune; patterns of communion are everywhere.

PART II
PLANETS AND EXTRATERRESTRIALS

4

INTELLIGENT BEINGS ON EARTH AND ON OTHER PLANETS

At one point in this universe that is racing outward, on a planet named Earth, there are intelligent animals. Are humans, women and men, the only planetary creatures in the cosmos with knowledge and freedom? Until recently, it had been presumed that Earth is unique, but the discovery of thousands of planets has changed that presumption.

These "exoplanets" come in a variety of sizes and compositions. Caleb Scharf writes,

> Next to living things, planets may be the most diverse and complex objects in the universe. No two planets are identical. All their properties are invariably variable....We know that there are at least as many planets as stars in our galaxy, and probably in the universe as a whole. In fact there are likely many more. The cosmos is teeming with exoplanets.[1]

In their search for planets, researchers have suggested that Earth-like planets would be common in some areas of the Milky Way. Alan Boss, for example, writes,

> All the evidence gathered to date by over ten years of planet hunting implies that Earth-like planets should be common in our neighborhood of the Milky Way Galaxy, and, by inference, in other galaxies as well. How common is common? Will essentially every nearby Sun-like star have a planet where an intelligent culture unfolds? Will 1 in 10 have such; or 1 in 100; or 1 in 1000?[2]

We are concerned here with planets orbiting distant stars and inhabited by intelligent peoples. The object of this consideration is not "UFOs." Those visitations, with their suspicious terrestrial characteristics, attained some prominence in the 1950s. No contact was verified. Because of the enormous distances between stars such are unlikely.

RELIGIOUS QUATERNITY

To be a person is to be searching for an explanation of the world. Like science, faith and religion ponder the universe. Mature religion accepts its limitations: a cloud of unknowing accompanies intimations of the divine.

The probability of exoplanets with intelligent societies implies religious faiths elsewhere. There are no reasons, scientific or religious, to think that Earth is the only place with a divine presence and message. John Haught finds religion to be composed of expressions of divine revelation, personal spirituality, social transformation, morality, and happiness.[3] These four realities appear basic and constant: (1) the knowing and free person; (2) a special contact by God beyond but within human nature; (3) evil and sin; and (4) time and history. Most of what human beings call religion or revelation, covenant or grace, involves what these realities represent and describe. They are very much the subject of Christianity.

The Knowing and Free Individual

Life displays a tendency to evolve toward more complex forms; some would reach levels of consciousness. On Earth, intellect has a specific corporeal life. Human life exists within the self-realization of a being who is corporality vivified by spirit. The characteristics of this material body are essentially related to its animating principle, and vice versa. This knowing animal can be considered medically and biologically, psychologically, and socially. Thomas Aquinas emphasized that the terrestrial "soul" is created by God not as an independent spirit but as the vivifying principle of a body. "The human being is not just a soul."[4]

Today, the field of bioastronomy studies the possible multitude of living species. Scientists ponder unusual life-forms like plasma, life in solid hydrogen, radiant life, and life in neutron stars as possible corporeal homes of knowing and loving. Timothy Harris observes,

> Life thrived on Earth for billions of years before land plants appeared and populated the continents. Biological evolution is so inherently unpredictable that even if life originated on a planet identical to Earth at the same time as it did here, life on that planet today would almost certainly be very different from terrestrial life.[5]

Those forms of intellect would have their own kinds of knowing, insight, instinct, and memory. Varied planetary lives are the background for thinking about the universe in wider ways, thinking about possible further knowledge about its source, "God," and might receive and believe in further forms of life called "salvation," and "life after death." Nancy Abrams and Joel Primack note that human beings on Earth, young and old, educated and uneducated, need to be introduced to their places in a particular galaxy with planetary civilizations. They should see how an individual on a planet or in a solar system retains identity and dignity. "A cosmic education would be a source of confidence and wisdom, a unifying outlook....Earth itself is not a mess but a jewel of the cosmos, rich with life and potential, and possibly unique in all the heavens....We are at the center of a new universe and at a pivotal moment for humanity."[6]

Special Contact by God

God's life touches humans in several ways. Christian faith is not basically about whether God exists, nor is it an indoctrination into religious rituals. Jesus called a special contact with God on Earth "the kingdom of God"; St. Paul named it "life in the Holy Spirit." In the Middle Ages, Aquinas wrote, "The human being is destined for a happiness beyond creation and nature, and so it needs to attain to higher realms....The gift of grace does not proceed from the light of nature but is added to it, bestowing a higher modality of activities."[7] In intelligent beings, creation and grace are distinct and yet interactive. If an intelligence can affirm analogously a few metaphysical ideas about a Creator, a person can, aided by God, accept a revelation of a deeper reality of divine love.

Some schools of Christian theology presume that intelligence and social life usually prepare for and lead to this higher, shared life. Karl Rahner's theology of the knowing subject and its history sees a deeper presence from God as the normal goal of life in intelligent persons. He notes,

We tend to presuppose that the goal of the world consists in God's communicating himself to it. We presuppose that the whole dynamism which God has instituted at the very heart of the world's becoming by its self-transcendence (but beyond what constitutes nature) is always meant as the beginning and first step toward a mode [of] divine self-communication.[8]

Both finite intelligence and divine presence have their activities and goals...and their interplay.

Evil and Sin

Evil is all too present on Earth, from the abuse of children to dictators' wars. Evil assumes several forms on Earth; terrestrial religion presumes widespread evil and deliberate sins. There are physical evils like illness and death, floods, and storms. There is also freely practiced human violence toward others; sins are personal, moral realizations of evil harming others. Not only do individual acts injure people, but on this planet, there seems to be an atmosphere of violence, a persistent dynamic of injury, and a social proclivity toward injustice and pain—"original sin." Does evil ordinarily exist elsewhere in the cosmos? Perhaps not. It might be infrequent, rare, even nonexistent. If evil exists in other worlds, however, it might have its own forms. Elsewhere in the universe, beings with free choice would easily avoid morally bad, injurious choices. Few civilizations would experience sin.

Science fiction often presents extragalactic worlds as hostile, violent, and predatory. There is no need to think that evil is as prominent in the universe as is nature or grace. We do not honor God by projecting on exoplanets Earth's proneness to violence. This would limit divine wisdom and power active in other civilizations.

Time and History

There is solar time, galactic time, and atomic time. There is the brief time of the existence of a muon and the lengthy time of the birth of a star. There are cultural ages for the arts like painting or musical composition—baroque, impressionist, postmodern. The universe's many temporalities do not just measure time but empower the inhabitants of the cosmos to fashion their politics and sciences. Intelligent existence implies the consciousness of time, of several times, and of times to be discovered. People experience time as outer (the motion of celestial bodies), cultural (the styles of architectures), and interior (a personal moment).

Penetrated by times, the entire cosmos, and not just Earth with the human race, will have its distinctive characteristics of history, past drama, and future creativity. There might, however, be planets with little change, with very slow revolutions and orbits. Other planets may neglect the past or let the present overshadow the future. What would these temporalities of cultures, renewal, and transformation on other planets be like?

EXOPLANETS

The last years of the twentieth century saw the discovery of exoplanets orbiting suns. The number has now reached more than six thousand. Earth is part of a galaxy with a long history, although any technology for contacting other planets is from the past hundred years. Knowledge of the worlds of the universe is coming to Earth not only through light but through ultraviolet and radio waves. Installations in California, Hawaii,

Puerto Rico, Chile, and Australia are examining stars to look for planets, while satelite telescopes focus on finding exoplanets. Tens of thousands of stars have been targeted as likely to have planets. If there are two hundred billion stars in the Milky Way and if 10 percent of them have planets, there are around twenty billion planets in this one galaxy. Among those planets supporting life in the average galaxy some of them would have self-organizing systems in brains and so an intellectual animality. William Stoeger asks, "A further—highly controversial issue—is the question of the origin of intelligent life in the universe. Is this highly probable, or improbable? Is the universe teeming with intelligent life, or are we a highly exceptional outcome of the action of physical laws?"[9] Planets with intelligent life, if they are even a small fraction of those in galaxies, would be numerous.

Understanding Earth—its size and location, its physical characteristics, and its biosphere—supports this quest. Other civilizations may have originated in the same area of star birth that gave rise to us, or they might exist in regions millions of light years away. Their forms of life might be startling on other worlds just from within Earth's galaxy, the Milky Way. And beyond that one galaxy there are millions of others.[10] Jacques Arnould concludes,

> The plurality of worlds, the existence of extraterrestrial intelligence is, in fact, a challenge on an encyclopedic scale. It raises both doubt and affirmation; it is surrounded by not only ideas from the past but by creations of human imagination today. It began with early philosophies but is now illumined by the results of the first exploration of space that can be called interplanetary.[11]

EXOPLANETARY RELIGION

The great variety of the stars and the possibility of life-forms on some of their planets suggest unsuspected directions in the realms of cultures and religions. Paul Wason writes,

> Part of being an intelligent, purposive agent is a deeply evolved ability to recognize the work of other intelligent, purposive agents, even, perhaps if they are not from planet Earth. It would work equally well the other way around, for any intelligent being will be a purposive agent and will therefore have evolved under conditions favoring the ability to recognize other agents and distinguish their work from other forms of causation.[12]

For theologians the reality of planetary intelligence introduces the probability of further faiths and religions. Perhaps they occur abundantly in the universe. Planets in distant galaxies and solar systems would have their own revelations, their own liturgies emerging in a colorful variety. They would have their versions of the religious quaternity.

The Knowing Person

Astrobiology and astrotheology invite speculation concerning structures of knowing and loving on worlds far away. On Earth, there are about eight million species of plants, animals, fungi, and algae, and there are billions of kinds of proteins. Astrochemists, as they explore the great sea of molecules in space, find new compounds with surprising atomic structures. Not a few scientists think that once life originates, the evolution of complex, intelligent life forms of some sort will unfold. Carl Sagan observes, "There is no reason to think that there is only one path to intelligent life. The selective advantage of intelligence is clearly high."[13] An extraterrestrial might be quite different from terrestrial animals and humans—the corporeal form minute in size or composed of unusual combinations of chemicals. Around 1700, Christiaan Huygens wrote, "Nor does it follow that they must be of the same shape as ours. There is such an infinite, but possible, variety of figures to be imagined that both the economy of these bodies and activities in their parts may be quite distinct, quite different from ours."[14] Planets would have their own evolutionary dynamics.

Extremophiles are a group of organisms that thrive in harsh environments on Earth like scalding water, subzero temperatures, extreme pressures, or the absence of oxygen and sunlight. Jo Marchant observes how life is more flexible, tenacious, and successful than previously thought:

> Bacteria have been found living in frigid, briny lakes beneath Antarctic ice and also deep within the superheated rocks of the Earth's crust. Entire ecosystems glean their energy not from sunlight, as once thought universal, but from chemical energy deep inside the planet. Bacteria can thrive in conditions of high acid, extreme gravity, crushing pressures or harsh radiations. Tiny but tough invertebrates called tardigrades have laid eggs in the near vacuum of space. Each new discovery has expanded our notion of life and, in turn, made it easier to imagine that it could have evolved elsewhere.[15]

Astrobiology is studying how life-forms could exist in challenging conditions of temperature and pressure. An extraterrestrial may thrive on intense energy, temperature, and pressure. Suns and planets can lead not solely to rapid explosions of gases and minerals but to more developed natural ecologies.

A planetary life communicating in its own languages could be like that of Earth or very different. They could suggest unknown aspects of the Ultimate. How do they see the divine plan for themselves in this cosmic community or in future transformation? Other civilizations may not only have their forms of astronomy and mathematics but their styles of literature and liturgy. Haught notes, "It is clear that the universe has always been dissatisfied with the monotony of the status quo, and so it has produced innumerable instances of ordered novelty."[16] Terrestrial imagination may not be able to approach even a small culture among the galaxies because of their diversity. "What we call intelligent life might turn out to be too trivial a notion to capture what is already 'out there,' or the incalculable cosmic outcomes that may yet occur in the future of this unfinished universe.... Intelligence in the evolving cosmos fashions its worlds."[17] Bob Berman suggests the ordinary survey of the planets not be solely determined by objects. Although telescopes grasp inhospitable and uninhabited rocks of ice and minerals, nature also aims very much and more deeply at consciousness. He states, "To those who see the cosmos as fundamentally consciousness-based, questions about shape and temperature are the wrong questions. Rather material nature will be the background for consciousness. It is primary and present in other (countless) ways."[18] Michael Ashkanazi has written a detailed study of possibilities for extraterrestrials ranging from bodily life and sensation to modes of intelligence and different kinds of language. He looks at their hypothetical planetary legal systems, aesthetics, and art forms and notes that the distances of other intelligent beings from each other are considerable, and yet some similarities could unfold.[19]

The vastness of the universe should not distract from appreciating the individual. It is the individual—tiger and tulip, composer and parent—who exists. Each being in its individuality and concrete nature has an identity, and this gives glory to God as the gift of his love and limitless art. This will be true for each planet. Stoeger concludes,

> The behavior of extraterrestrials—as well as the realities of natural and moral evil and suffering—might be completely different among them. But, whatever their biologies, they would be based on the very same physics and chemistry as ours is, including the second law of thermodynamics. Each individual in each kind of person would have its fragility and its transcendence.[20]

A Special Contact

Most people on Earth believe that some revelation comes to them from and about God. It is silent, personal, implicit, and is usually socially expressed. It includes empowerment by God for morality and future life.[21] Christianity holds that the God creating intelligent beings on Earth decided to be the source of a deeper life for these beings. Is that true on other planets? Does intelligence ordinarily receive a further divine presence? Always? On the one hand, through a personal life joined to prudence and freedom, intelligence might exist only in its natural state on some planets. On the other hand, planetary pluralism could have its own ideas of election, covenant, sanctity. This or that intelligent creature, far away from us, could receive special life and information from God. Divine love for the entire cosmic community would be itself a revelation not easily grasped. As Haught notes, "What seems to be universally applicable…is the idea of embracing rather than eliminating diversity….Terrestrial religions, as they contact other 'cultures,' will provide fresh challenges and also opportunities for growth."[22] In distant civilizations, there might be more knowledge about the plans of God for the universe and its peoples. What would happen to terrestrial theologies when confronted with languages of faith from other planets?[23] Encounters with new kinds of religion would bring enrichment to Earth's traditions and faiths. Other intelligent species may have specific theologies of how they and their societies are friends or companions of God through symbols, icons, ideas. It is likely that there are many bands on the spectrum of supernatural life for creatures and not just one form. There would be cosmic ecumenism.

Evil

As we noted earlier, evil presents itself in various forms: natural disasters, illnesses, violence, and destruction. Evil might not infect an entire species on this or that planet; it might not even touch the race, the society, the collectivity. An intelligent race might not be involved with personal wrongdoing.

Some philosophers, devout believers, scientists, and artists see evil as a concomitant result of intelligence and freedom. Choices for violence toward others result directly just from being intelligent and free.[24] There are religious traditions with a preference for the apocalyptic, for disaster, for suffering, for terminal destruction, for the ends of worlds. This negative sectarianism is neither particularly Christian nor clearly human. Faith and theology need not project Earth's proneness to evil and violence onto other planetary cultures. There is no need to think that evil is more prominent in the universe than being, life, or grace.

Scientists themselves can be negative, using a language of violence when describing ordinary cosmic processes. Stephen Hawking and other secular thinkers find it wrongheaded to assume that extraterrestrials would be friendly. Meetings between Earth and another planet would be like that between the Spanish conquistadores and native Americans. Popular writings on astronomy frequently use metaphors of violence to describe nature's processes. There are "star wars." Old suns find "death in a black hole." Stars are "cannibalized" by a "monster" nebula; galaxies "bully" neighboring galaxies, "gobbling up" each other. One source for this projection of evil may be the deep-seated fear on Earth of others, as the usages in English of "aliens" show.

Evil is not an aspect of God's realms that are worlds born of degrees of love. Suffering and decline should not dominate the reality of life and incarnation; people exist for life, not death. The history of sin and salvation recorded in the two testaments of the Bible is a particular religious history on one planet and not the single framework or the sole history of God's contact with all civilizations in the universe. The crucifixion of Jesus on Earth is the result of terrestrial, religious, and political rejections of what is good. There can be creatures who have no propensity for deception and violence, races who do not choose what is against their reality and morality. Seth Shostak suggests that even for Earth the recent millennia with a preponderance of war and crime might be a temporary, short period in what is a lengthy human evolution, in the past and in the future.[25] A society might live out their cultural and political dimensions free of selfishness.[26]

In the science fiction series by C. S. Lewis from the last century, there are several planets with civilizations. Their people are benign and wise; they are in community with each other and with the divine. These planetarians, however, have no contact with Earth and no communication comes out of it. Sin has brought to it a cloud of isolation. The third novel concludes with an interplanetary assembly where civilizations—unhindered by great distances—express their identities and salvation histories. One planet is absent from this gathering: the "silent planet." To it no one travels and from it no one comes. Its "silence" comes from its special situation: it holds the reality and force, the presence and the enactment of evil.

45

The isolated, silent planet is "Earth."[27] Evil among planets, then, could be rare, quite exceptional.[28]

Time and History

Divine contact may come at the beginning of a culture, or it may come at the end. Or God may be present to creatures mainly in the present. Revelation might occur in a few instants or emerge over millennia. Terrestrial historicity is only one temporality; other civilizations will have their own times and consequently their own histories of revelation recorded in their cultures. Those frameworks might have little to do with history, as Earth understands it. God's presence in a specific world suits the people to which it comes. Fulfillment comes at the end of their time. Civilizations evolve forward, drawn to what is deeper and creative, to what is richer in culture and science...and revelation. Some are destined far in the future to encounter other planets. Some may hold impetuses coming from divine life. A future chapter will look more closely at times and transfigurations.

Several chapters of this book consider extraterrestrials. Jacques Arnould concludes,

> Long before it was an issue for contemporary science this topic has stimulated theological, religious perspectives. Today new discoveries and wider probabilities make it not a question of theological anxiety or religious eccentricity but one that draws Christianity to reflect on its own depth and significance.[29]

5

TERRESTRIAL VIEWS OF PLANETARY PERSONS

Somewhere in space, billions of miles away, a strange-looking race of intelligent beings lives out a long history as they compose their technology, music, and literature. That imaginative scenario taking place is no longer a fantasy. With so many galaxies and planets transiting their stars, there may be many such civilizations. Historian Michael Crowe concludes his survey of theories about extraterrestrials in modern times by writing,

> Thus the locales available for extraterrestrials have increased, as have our knowledge of the universe and the power of our telescopic equipment. Were the authors [from the past] to return to life in the twentieth-first century, they would find an area known for over twenty centuries as the plurality of worlds transformed in techniques and title. Moreover, astronomy is pursued by thousands of scientists, enriched in tens of thousands of publications, and funded by many millions of dollars.[1]

We are at a special time in history, in science, in astrophysics, and in thinking about existence and the world.

ANALYSTS OF EXTRATERRESTRIALS

For centuries, people have imagined persons living on other celestial bodies. At times, their ideas were colored by religion. Over the last two thousand years, there have been Christian theologians who had no problem with the divine power creating intelligent beings on planets. What follows is a selection of their theories about extraterrestrials.

Origen (184–253), author of the first Christian systematic theology, pondered time and matter, stars and angels. They were part of the world being studied at the library and university in Alexandria, Egypt, in the decades before, during, and after his lifetime. Much earlier, in the fourth century BCE, the philosopher and religious thinker Epicurus wrote that "there are an almost infinite number of worlds, some like ours and some quite different."[2] For him, the composition of matter by atoms allows through their minuteness the production of beings beyond Earth's solar system. The theologian Origen described God's creation as a movement leading to intelligent creatures. Of different kinds, they were absorbed in the contemplation of God. Their attention wandered, however, and through that declining contemplation they fell away from their pristine state. They fell in varying degrees, and the degree of fall gave diversity to angels and demons in power and existence and diversified human beings in sensual animality.[3] Nonetheless, a journey forward to God is offered to all knowing beings. On various inhabited stars and planets, they live and learn, and so become more knowledgeable and mature. Spiritual lives grow on their paths before and after death, paths to remarkable future ways of life.

Guillaume de Vaurouillon (ca. 1392–1463) developed a positive theology of extraterrestrials in the contours of the spirituality of the Friars Minor. Already in the thirteenth century, Bonaventure, the biographer of Francis of Assisi and author of speculative and mystical texts, wrote that God could have made other worlds: "He was able to make a hundred such worlds, one at a higher level than another, and, still more, one embracing all of them. And too God could make a time before this time and in it make a world."[4] After attaining a doctorate and attending the Council of Basel, Vaurouillon lectured at the University of Paris on theology.[5] He wrote that God could create many worlds: "Infinite worlds, more perfect than this one, lie hid in the mind of God."[6] These worlds would have their own geological and biological forms. "It is possible that the species of each of these worlds is different from those of our world."[7] He did not, however, imagine knowledge from those worlds ever coming to men and women on Earth, for they are too distant; only angelic communication or some special divine action could make humans aware of them.

Vaurouillon looked at the role of Jesus Christ in this wider universe with reserve and insight. Another world would have its own revelation, sin, and redeemer, or none of these. Other worlds with intelligent beings are not necessarily implicated in our world of sin. They do not need a savior or a divine prophet coming from another world. "If it be inquired whether people, existing on that world, have sinned as Adam sinned, I answer, No. They would not have contracted sin just as their humanity is not from Adam."[8] If there is no primal, terrestrial original sin, there need not be redemption from it. Jesus Christ, hypostatically related to the Word, would not move from planet to planet. "As to the question whether Christ by dying on this Earth could redeem the inhabitants of another world, I answer that he was able to do this not only for our world but for infinite worlds. However, it would not be fitting for him to go to another world to die again."[9] When one real incarnation occurs, it occurs in one precise species.

TOWARD A COSMIC THEOLOGY

Vaurouillon's theological distinctions concerning extra-terrestrials make him a pioneer. He is an intermediary between some Scholastics of the thirteenth and fourteenth centuries who declared that God could in theory create a plurality of worlds and the philosophers of science in the sixteenth and later centuries who asserted that God had indeed created theologically distinct forms of personhood and salvation history for other planets.

Giordano Bruno (1548–1600) set aside his life of clois-tered Scholasticism as a Dominican in Naples, in 1579, to seek his fortune in northern Europe. Metaphysician more than theo-logian, astronomer but also magician and poet, he lived in academic societies in Geneva, London, and Wittenberg. In those Protestant theological centers, contrary to what was expected, he encountered a lack of intellectual freedom and hostility toward his ideas. He established himself in Venice, hoping to find tolerance and a position at the University of Padua (a chair that was twenty years later given to Galileo). Prone to dramatic statements and activities, he was arrested in Venice, in 1592, and then imprisoned in Rome for several years. He was tried and executed for religious reasons like the use of magic, negative views of Jesus's relationship to God and human salvation, and his rejection of the eucharistic presence. He was not executed for his affirmation of an infinite universe nor for his view that there are intelligent creatures elsewhere in the universe. In times when science, philosophy, faith, and theology were too intertwined, his lasting contributions got lost in religious eccentricity and ecclesiastical violence.

Bruno taught that the universe is infinite and living; it holds many worlds of which Earth is only one. The stars occupy the pinnacle of a hierarchy of living things; some of them have forms of knowledge and freedom. In addition to these stellar beings, he populated planets with individuals, for sciences and the biblical books refer to thousands of other intelligent creatures.[10] Participation in divine life can be given widely. For these other intelligent creatures, incarnations in their races are possible. However, scholars have observed that in some ways the animated celestial bodies—corporeal and intelligent, varied and interactive—rather replace the incarnation of the Logos on Earth and elsewhere in the universe.

The Enlightenment

In the sixteenth century, the Reformers emphasized the biblical life of Jesus and the terrestrial corruption of sin and discouraged considering other peoples. Liberal Protestant theologies left Calvin and Luther for a philosophical, deist direction with a supreme being presiding over a moral society. In the following centuries the Enlightenment pursued ethics and theodicy in a simple and universal religion, and some thinkers discussed races on planets and stars.

For *Thomas Paine* (1737–1809), the universe is filled with creatures in the way that Earth is filled with living beings, and so it is likely that a supreme being has populated planets. That chain of worlds is not subject to a cloud of original sin, nor does it need redemptions and incarnations. "Are we to suppose that every world in the boundless creation had an Eve, an apple, a serpent, and a redeemer? In this case the person who is irreverently called the Son of God, and sometimes God himself, would have nothing else to do than to travel from world to world, in an endless succession of deaths, with scarcely a momentary interval of life."[11] Paine states some of the contradictions that arise from projecting a simplistic Christology onto the universe. In 1733, *Alexander Pope* (1688–1744), a leading English poet of the first decades of the eighteenth century, imagined other planets instructing Earth:

He, who through vast immensity can pierce,
See worlds on worlds compose one universe,
Observe how system into system runs,
What other planets circle other suns.[12]

Ralph Waldo Emerson (1803–1882) held that because Christianity is fading, a new religion was needed, one teaching "no expiation by Jesus…no mysterious relations to him. It will teach great, plain, eternal truths."[13] To address those involved in modern physics and philosophy, Christianity should present Jesus as "the gracious instrument of [God's] bounty to instruct men in the character of God and the true nature of spiritual good."[14] Clearly, there are other races in the cosmos—ethical and enlightened peoples—and they do not need an incarnation. Emerson delivered a sermon in May of 1832 asking how a person could be a Calvinist given modern astronomy. After stating that the Earth is not the center of the universe and observing that other creatures may not resemble humans, he found it likely that, in the universe, there are "inhabitants of other worlds."[15] God and the moral law are a universal religion, not incarnation.

In the following century, academic thinkers like Hegel, Feuerbach, and Schelling rejected ideas of inhabited planets, while sectarian and fundamentalist churches affirmed them. As the twentieth century began, it was recognized that thinkers had fashioned hypotheses about persons on other celestial bodies for well over two thousand years.

CONTEMPORARY THEOLOGIANS AND EXTRATERRESTRIALS

In the twentieth century, there were Catholic theologians who accepted the possibility of planetary societies. At the same time, most rejected the idea that the Logos in Jesus of Nazareth would visit or save other races. God can initiate various ways of contacting and assisting other peoples in their own histories. In 1952, an Italian Jesuit, Domenico Grasso, wrote,

> Knowledge of extraterrestrials would help us penetrate the wisdom of the plans of God and the evil of sin. If they live in a state of justice they would not have committed original sin, and we would see the immensity of all that was lost by our ancestors through sin. In cases resembling a redemption like ours we would see the special love of God for us in terms of a further experience of this love for others.[16]

At that time, his preliminary considerations had been stimulated by reports of UFOs. He did not link these possible peoples to sin, the need for redemption, or having contact with Jesus of Nazareth. That enthusiastic time of extraterrestrial observation and fantasy soon faded.

In the second half of the twentieth century, *Karl Rahner* (1904–84) fashioned a theology both speculative and existential, subject centered and historical. He looked at dozens of issues in religion, and already in 1964, the German Jesuit theologian had published an article on "star-inhabitants." People on Earth are now aware that they are living on a tiny planet that is part of a system of a particular sun that itself belongs to its own galaxy of stars. Noting the great distance of other stars from us, he suggested that this issue has little to do with our personal existence and belief. Extraterrestrials, however, would not inhabit bizarre jungles or underwater cities but would live in their own worlds—in the modern sense of "world." They would be distinguished in an important way not by their location in the cosmos but by "their intellectual subjectivity determining the reality of space and time,"[17] for example, by social, cultural, and existential forms.

How does one combine the discoveries of science about life in space with the assertions of theology about a unique place for the human race? In 1983, the Jesuit theologian wrote a longer reflection on intelligent beings of other celestial bodies. A dynamic and evolving universe has as one of its goals the development of life to the point of intelligent consciousness. Rahner notes, "It would be excessively anthropomorphic to view the Creator-God as directing cosmic evolution at another location in the universe to the point where the immediate possibility of free and intellectual life is present but then casually breaking off that development."[18] God is free to fashion other worlds of different types. Christian faith and theology should not reject but encourage histories of free intelligence on other planets.

Are not intelligent forms of life existing in other planetary systems also touched by God's more intense presence and plans? Civilizations of extraterrestrials are likely given some revelation and assistance from a special self-communication of God. "We presuppose, therefore, that the goal of the world consists in God's communicating himself to it. We presuppose that the whole dynamism which God has instituted at the very heart of the world's becoming by [its] self-transcendence (and also beyond what constitutes nature) is always meant as the beginning and first step toward this divine self-communication."[19] God's vitalization flows through cultural and religious forms. Does the evolution of an intellectual race within shared divine life lead to incarnation? It could. "In terms of the immutability of God in God-self and in the selfhood of the Logos one certainly cannot prove that a pluriform incarnation in various histories of salvation is simply inconceivable."[20] Both matter and spirit aim at development, and that dynamic brings concrete realizations in the galaxies. Respect for a future always developing suggests a modest openness to what awaits. Rahner states, "Theologians will not say more about this issue than to indicate that Christian revelation has as its goal the salvation of human beings. It does not give answers to questions which have no importance for the realization of this salvation in terrestrial freedom."[21]

Jacques Arnould (b. 1961), theologian at France's Centre National d'Études Spatiales, affirms a creativity in God capable of unfolding endless forms in the cosmos. Are the millions of species on Earth an intimation of the varied populations of the galaxies? Theology and astronomy are discovering and contemplating the reality of intelligent life in the cosmos. Arnould notes that "creation is not understood as the present or the conservation of the past. It is a work in process, planned and sustained by the will of God. The life of extraterrestrials can be a gift for believers and theologians."[22] Positive interactions between peoples and planets could show the richness of the galaxies. Arnould meditates on other intelligences in the cosmos: "These races and peoples are our neighbors but different from us. Today they are unknown and inaccessible. We are alone. This solitude can bring forth three attitudes: to move away, to wait, or anticipate....The third stance is eminently theological."[23] What lies ahead is not frightening or chaotic when we recall that the universe is huge, varied, and ordered.

Armin Kreiner (b. 1954), professor at the Ludwig Maximilians University in Munich, looks at possible connections between extraterrestrials and human religions. Clearly, not everything important about God and creation has been stated by the Bible. Other worlds might be closer to God's life; revelation to a planet orbiting three suns might be unhampered by an atmosphere of ignorance and selfishness. A cosmic religion is "an encounter with the Spirit of the Creator. Seeing the universe filled with signs and effects of the divine is not a possession of Earthlings. There is a wider, unfolding, and varied wisdom for all planetary intelligences."[24] Far from being constraining, Christian theologies can fashion astrotheologies with psychologies of mysticism and sacramentality. The German theologian concludes that Christians need to see extraterrestrial religions in a broader perspective, one that would go beyond terrestrial salvation history with its Christology. While Jesus the Christ is central to graced life on Earth through one incarnational reality of the Word, there could be hypostatic realizations on other planets. Kleiner notes, "It is shortsighted and ignorant to ignore the ET issue any longer. It touches not just upon pure possibilities but realities. For even if the contact with an ET never happens, still its very possibility contributes ideas about the self-understanding of Christianity."[25] Gradually, the universe will offer new ways to approach the divine, its presence and messages, salvation histories, and cosmic eschatologies.

John Haught (b. 1942), a prolific writer in theology, culture, and science, has published an incipient cosmic theology, noting that both astrophysics and Christian theologies are in their beginnings. He notes that traditions of theology are waiting to be drawn forward by analyses of galaxies and solar systems and concludes that "if interstellar travel ever occurs, contact with extraterrestrial 'cultures' will provide fresh challenges and opportunities for growth."[26] God is at work in planetary civilizations in the planned fields of the universe, and they, rooted in an ultimate unity of being, point to a Source.[27] The rigidity of Romanesque metaphysics and baroque liturgy are being replaced by the dynamics suggested by galaxies. Most likely, revelation expands through planetary salvation histories and theologies where intelligences are fashioning their worlds and religions. Human faith becomes less about past rituals and more about future lives. Anticipation is today's eschatology. "Aware that the cosmic story is far from over, it looks patiently and expectantly ahead for a possible meaning to all....Something significant is working itself out in the universe now as in the past. It reads the cosmic story in both scientific and religious terms, from outside and inside simultaneously."[28] With Jesus's teaching about religious and social change and his prototypical resurrection, Christianity is very much about anticipating further times and realms. All extraterrestrials are personalized intersections between religion and astrophysics. Haught sees *convergence* rather than *contrast* to be the milieu of meeting galactic civilizations: "What must their own life and intelligence be like in order to allow us to share ideas about God or salvation."[29]

Douglas Vakoch (b. 1961) began as a psychologist and historian of science, interested in the religious reactions on Earth as people ponder extraterrestrials. He became a founder of the Search for Extraterrestrial Intelligence (SETI) Institute, which studies the phenomenon of extraterrestrial life. Their main project is launching attempts to contact extraterrestrials through repeated messages sent toward the vicinity of a star. So far, none of these searches has yielded evidence of return signals from extraterrestrial intelligence. Distance challenges contacts: sending a message from one edge of our galaxy to another takes two hundred thousand years. Extraterrestrial beings using different scientific theories and models of the basic composition of the universe might have a different way of representing things, and so to them terrestrial pictograms would not be clear.

Vakoch has founded a similar organization, Messaging Extraterrestrial Intelligence (METI) to conduct scientific research and educational programs promoting international cooperation and collaboration in understanding the societal implications of searching for life beyond Earth. METI and SETI look for pulses coming from advanced civilizations; they seek to contact planets around stars by mathematical or chemical formulae sent out repeatedly. METI targets nearby stars and considers a suitable medium and message to send them. Conferences about interstellar contacts build an interdisciplinary community to design interstellar messages. Civilizations with advanced technologies would have high levels of culture in many areas. Over the last twenty years, the chances have improved of exoplanets being found, and it seems likely that perhaps twenty percent of the planets being discovered move in a zone suitable for life-forms.

For Vakoch, the popular view of "hostile aliens" is unlikely. On the one hand, their arts might be surprisingly helpful and aggressive orientations would be rare. On the other hand, they might not be interested in contacting civilizations at our level or in our region of this galaxy because those interests may have been pursued a billion years earlier and saw no signs of life.

Guy Consolmagno, SJ (b. 1952), is the president of the Vatican Observatory Foundation and the head of its educational institute. As a scientist, he studies meteorites and asteroids. Conflicts between science and religion are fading, he observes, while the very progress of science leads to more questions for scientists. The Jesuit has no doubt that life and intelligent life exist elsewhere in the universe. When humanity learns of extraterrestrials, the news will come as no big surprise. The likely discovery—whether next month or a millennium from now—will be received much the way that the news of planets orbiting far off stars has been absorbed since the 1990s. Faith and theology are not closed collections of terms and propositions but ways of learning more about the universe.

EXTRATERRESTRIALS AND RELIGION

Civilizations with advanced technologies would have high levels of culture in many areas, and planetary views on religion will be expressed in their thought forms, languages, and arts. Verbal contacts with other peoples could be complicated, perhaps barely possible. John Haught recalls this: "What must their own life and intelligence be like in order to allow us to share ideas about God or salvation."[30] It might not be simple for us to explain our religious beliefs or for them to explain theirs. The discovery of life elsewhere will neither prove nor disprove the existence of God; it will open the door to pondering what form salvation history assumes in other intelligent societies.

Theology like astrophysics invites considerations of life and intelligence in worlds far away. Planets may be at the beginning or end of their histories of intelligence and of grace. Their meditative view of God may emphasize specific realities. What seem central to religions on Earth—sin, guilt, sacrifice, appeasement—may not exist and may be difficult for other planets to understand. The divine can set in motion many projects and peoples…and many disclosures of itself.

6

INCARNATIONS

Men and women seek to contact an invisible presence that is also an unseen but believed-in transcendent reality. Many religions on Earth, proclaimed and celebrated by priests and peoples, affirm God to be acting within human persons and their communities. The divine is at work in billions of terrestrial men and women beyond science, art, political movements, and personal life in what is called "religion," "mysticism," and "liturgy."

One religious presence, however, has a special intensity. Here the divine finds a distinctive expression; it appears in, indeed becomes, a concrete individual of a particular race. That union and interplay is called an "incarnation." Christians believe that in a special way human searching meets divine revelation in one human: Jesus of Nazareth. The divine is uniquely present in one fully human being: the Word of God as the Son of Mary and of Joseph.[1]

CHRISTIAN PERSPECTIVES ON INCARNATION

Incarnation is a special divine presence flowing into and through the totality of one free, intelligent being. Early

Christians—their teachers and opponents—understood that the newness and shock of the message of Christianity was not that God was appearing on Earth (the theme of many picturesque religious myths and fables), but that the unique God had become psychologically and socially one human being in this world. God, active through the Word of the triune God, is present in one individual living out of a species, Jesus, son of Joseph. "Word" in Greek means not just an element of language but a "plan," a project, a pattern. For Christians, it means the second divine facet of God at work in the cosmos. Opening the Gospel according to John with its view of the Trinity is the line, "And the Word became flesh" (John 1:14). The Greek text then states literally that the Word "pitched his tent among us."[2] God did not just appear on Earth for a few weeks or assume a bodily shell. The divine lived a human life as Jesus of Nazareth, as one who "pitched his tent" among the human tribe moving through history with its religions and cultures. His life and teaching in a Semitic religious world and a Roman political one sought to bring to Earth God's reign as a society of love in both a present and future life.

In the centuries after Jesus, Christian theologians in the Roman and Byzantine empires fashioned a metaphysical anthropology to support both oneness and interplay between the divine sphere and the human individual. They gave Greek philosophical definitions to person, nature, existence, divine person, and human individuality. Ecclesial councils stated how three central realities—human nature, divine nature, and divine person—meet in Jesus. Drawn from the language and philosophy of the Hellenistic age, "person" meant the metaphysical point of origin and organization in one individual; it has little to do with modern ideas of person and personality. These Greek theological and metaphysical traditions limited how incarnation was understood in Christian churches in subsequent centuries. Jesus is fully a human being and also the active presence of the Word of God in an autonomous individual. Yves Congar underlined a lasting problem: "We know that Jesus Christ is God. But how is God Jesus Christ?"[3]

An incarnation is not a miracle or a magic show. Incarnation means a divine modality in this individual of a species. Some Christians have not infrequently placed too much emphasis on the divine in Jesus as if it is the one important causal reality in him. In the past, groups have asserted that an incarnation is a mixture of the human and the divine or that the human is a channel or a shell for the divine. Others have overemphasized a Son of God in a human body replacing the brain or soul. In modern periods, some theologians set aside the divine presence altogether, and Jesus becomes a special teacher and solely human. The point of incarnation, however, is divine presence in the finite person; it is not the reduction of either of them or the product of their mixture. Furthermore, incarnation is distinct from redemption, an activity by the incarnate one that compensates for and removes the sinfulness of men and women. If sin on other planets is limited or nonexistent, incarnation, nonetheless, remains valuable, for it is illustrative and educative; it need not be involved in a form of suffering redemption.

Christianity is always struggling to affirm a true incarnation: totally Jesus and extensively the Word of God. Speculation about extraterrestrial religions and psychologies, information on the vast extent of the universe, an awareness of minute and singularly active particles and waves—these can reveal new considerations of ways that the divine could be present in a created individual—an incarnation.

EXTRATERRESTRIALS AND INCARNATIONS

The possibility of incarnations on other planets has been raised by Christians and by believers from other religions. Some of the thinkers who affirmed the possibility of incarnation elsewhere have already been presented in the preceding pages. Interestingly, little more than a century after Bethlehem, Christian theologians considered possible further modes of incarnation beyond Jesus of Nazareth. The divine would bring an intense presence in terms of intelligent creatures on other stars or planets.

Origen (184–253), as we saw, thought that the stars and planets visible in the sky are alive although they exist in different ways from humans and angels.[4] Stars are primal intelligences in fiery forms, while planets and the moon are heavenly material bodies with populations enjoying life. As the universe has a breadth of beings of matter and intelligence, the divine Word (who was for a time incarnate on Earth in Jesus of Nazareth) has a wider incarnational presence. This divine being comes to various worlds in their proper forms. The Logos acquires an angelic condition among angels, just as among people on Earth it acquired a human individuality. The trinitarian persons become incarnate in stellar and planetary races. With this theology, Origen located the biblical life and work of Jesus on Earth in a drama that was cosmic.[5]

Thomas Aquinas (1225–1274) presented God not as a supreme being or a judge but as an all-active limitless and timeless Reality. Motivated by generosity to create and sustain other beings, God intends a universe that is diverse and imaginatively arranged. Wisdom and love impel divine plans into external realizations. "God is a living fountain, one not diminished in spite of its continuous flow outwards."[6] The motive for both creation and incarnation is goodness diffusing itself by bestowing life on others. Incarnation is an intense way for God to be present to a community of creatures and to communicate with them. Aquinas notes,

> To be a human being is truly predicated of God here.
> At the same time this is not an eternal attribute of

God but one that arises in time with the assumption
of a human nature....With a human nature God does
not acquire a new personal existence but simply a
new relation of his already existing personal existence to this human nature.[7]

This medieval thinker, like Aristotle before him, prized
an overarching unity in the universe giving place and order
to each reality. That single unity in the cosmos finds support
from faith as well as from science.[8] Aquinas noted that there
are some who have posited a number of worlds, those cosmologies, implying chance and disorder, neglect the network and
relationship between the celestial lights we see. The Dominican saw one world and so one incarnation. At the same time,
Franciscan and some cathedral schools held the possibility of
a plurality of worlds, now and in other times.[9]

For a careful thinker like Aquinas, the humanity of Jesus
of Nazareth remains finite, minute compared to the projects
of the all-powerful Word of God. The capabilities of a divine
person are infinite; they cannot be limited or focused on one
enterprise.

Could the Word of God be incarnate in creatures other
than Jesus of Nazareth? Aquinas said that it could be. The
incarnation on Earth is one divine activity. God is not enclosed
in Jesus of Nazareth. "The Son of God could have taken flesh
from whatever material reality it selected."[10] All three persons
can become incarnate, and incarnation is only one aspect of
boundless divine power. The inner life of the reality of God
surging out of three divine personal activities with the names
of Parent, Word, and Wind are not excluded from multiple
incarnations. Aquinas states,

If a divine person could not assume another [cre-
ated] nature, then the personal mode of the divine

nature would be enclosed by the one human nature. But it is impossible for the Uncreated to be circumscribed by the created. Whether we look at the divine person according to its power (which is the source of the union [with a finite nature]) or at its personhood (which is the term of the union [with a finite nature], one must say that the divine person beyond the human being that it has assumed can assume others of human nature.[11]

An incarnation of the eternal Word has occurred in one individual of the intelligent species on Earth. That enterprise of the Word unfolding in the life of a Jewish prophet hardly limits, exhausts, or curtails the divine Word's activity, real or potential.

Giordano Bruno (1548–1600) taught that the universe—infinite and living—holds many worlds of which Earth is one. The stars may be home to living creatures, and planets can have their own intelligent populations. Bruno's view is bold and creative:

This infinite world is the true subject and infinite material of the infinite divine actual potency. This was made to be well understood both by regulated reason and discourse and by divine revelations which state that there is no countable number of the ministers of the Most High, to whom thousands of thousands assist and ten hundreds of thousands administer. These are the great animals: many of these have a clear light emanating from their bodies, and are from all sides visible to us.[12]

Because there are other intelligent creatures, incarnations in their races are possible. Civilizations with incarnations would teach each other how the divine is more than a distant absolute or a deity localized in one set of sacral objects. Incarnation opens the particular to the divine. Civilizations with incarnations could teach each other to look further and to understand more.

Karl Rahner (1904–1984) saw creation and incarnation as two phases of the process of God's self-giving to others, both in being and in deeper life. The universe culminates in the creation of beings of intelligence, and so the possibility of the development of life to the point of intelligent consciousness in other galaxies cannot be excluded. The universe is not a natural park built by God for terrestrial men and women. It is a world of worlds permeated by times and evolutions.

In this theology, intelligent beings are normally (or always) invited to God's special friendship, "revelation" and "grace." "In the world, as it actually is, we can understand Creation and Incarnation as two moments and two phases of *one* process of God's self-giving and self-expression, although this is an intrinsically differentiated process."[13] The gift of God's self-disclosing friendship has a movement toward the concrete, the personal, toward the individual. An incarnation is an intensification of that grace present in all people on this or any other planet. The incarnate one has everything that belongs to being a finite person. Rahner wrote,

> [Incarnation] includes a limited subjectivity in which the world becomes conscious in its own unique, historically conditioned and finite way; and a subjectivity which has a radical immediacy to God in and through God's self-communication of God.[14]

This special divine presence could exist elsewhere in the cosmos. Different modes of trinitarian presence could be at work, going beyond grace and expressing incarnation. "In terms of the immutability of God in God-self and of the selfhood of the Logos, one certainly cannot prove that a pluriform incarnation in various histories of salvation is simply inconceivable."[15] Does the complexity of the cosmos not imply further incarnations?

INCARNATIONS ON DISTANT PLANETS

Cultural creativity on a particular planet fashions specific modes of divine presence and so may also lead dynamically to incarnations.[16] The fourth-century Egyptian theologian Athanasius of Alexandria, began his approach to Christian theology focused not on Jesus but on creation. God is present in creation in many ways. God is present in Jesus of Nazareth in an intense, personal way. This approach may lead to the expectation of incarnations in various kinds of beings in the universe, in clusters of stars with planets and moons there could be incarnations of the divine presence. The divine enters intimately into the physical and psychological reality of an intelligent species of a different modality. Its size may be small or large; its mental capacities may be unusual as might its memory and healthy willpower. Other planetary intelligent natures have their ecologies and psychologies, their modes of living and thinking. An incarnation is not a reproduction of Jesus of Nazareth with minor alterations; it is a concrete expression of the Ultimate vitalizing the life of a planetary knowing being. Each incarnation would take place in a specific intelligent species. There is no reason to think that these are rare.

Reflecting on incarnations in planetary races different from ours would lead terrestrial theologies to consider life, history, love, and society in new ways. Jacques Arnould sees incarnation as a planetary stimulus for theology: "In an analogous way, the work of Christ's redemption (his incarnation, his suffering, his resurrection) should be examined from the perspective of extraterrestrials as they would be existing."[17] Theologians have pointed out that there are kinds and degrees of interplays between the divine and the creaturely; and so too, kinds of incarnation. All this would reveal new anthropologies of grace for individuals.

One mode of incarnation exists in one planetary species. That incarnate being would not become incarnate elsewhere in a second species. God might send a messenger from one culture to another intelligent civilization, but this is not God incarnate in the second people. Different anthropologies, modes of intelligence, and kinds of communication may well make such a journey from planet to planet useless or impossible.

As we saw, C. S. Lewis wrote novels—*That Hideous Strength, Perelandra, Out of the Silent Planet*[18]—about extraterrestrials living on planets in Earth's solar system. They were living out their distinctive salvation histories: in 1913, just prior to those novels being written, the British poet Alice Meynell composed a poem about incarnation as a cosmic reality. The stars of the visible constellations hold societies and in them God becomes incarnate in one of their members. These different incarnations manifest the divine:

> But, in the eternities,
> Doubtless we shall compare together, hear
> A million alien Gospels, in what guise
> He trod the Pleiades, the Lyre, the Bear.
> Oh, be prepared, my soul!
> To read the inconceivable, to scan
> The million forms of God those stars unroll
> When, in our turn, we show to them a Man.[19]

In the poem, there are multiple incarnations, "forms of God," where the divine is individualized in planetary peoples. They bring their various "gospels," not a half dozen but a "million." A remarkable view for its time.

Incarnation can reach a variety of intelligent beings. A goal of the universe consists in God communicating higher modes of life to it, ones that can arrive on a planet in this or that stage of its evolution or history. Word or Spirit may have physically become a member of a distant race millions of years ago, or they may have become incarnate on a planet flourishing today. There could be galaxies whose planets are evolving toward colorful futures.

PART III
WORLDS AND TIMES

7

A SUBATOMIC WORLD AND DIVINE PRESENCE

Whatever little we can know about God comes from traces left in creation by a cause who is an artist. Thomas Aquinas wrote, "To the extent that a creature has existence it has some representations of the divine existence and the divine goodness."[1] The size of the universe and the variety of its beings represent myriad aspects of a breadth that is the divine.

MINUTE INTERACTIONS

God's deeper contacts and modes of presence—for instance, in religions on Earth—are called "revelation," "grace," "covenant," or "salvation." Human faith affirms that divine activity comes to people on Earth, bringing information about the sacral past, the problematic present, and the unknown future. Grace and revelation—what Jesus calls the "kingdom of God"—are a presence at work in men and women, a divine presence that is silent, subtle, and implicit in its contact with humans. Aquinas saw this special presence in people to be a further kind of life surpassing natural forms. Jesus called it the realm of God. Aquinas notes, "It is not suitable that God provide more for creatures being led by divine love to a natural good than for those creatures to whom that love offers a supernatural good."[2] Special modalities of life, deeper and stronger, hope filled and informative, come to men and women within and above human nature.

In the universe, evolution in life probably leads to intelligent creatures, and intelligent life normally calls forth God's friendship.[3] Cosmic forces, subatomic particles, kinds of bosons may suggest theologies of that divine activity. Matthias Remenyi observes, "God's contact with his creation never remains a purely external contact. In the age of eschatological completion God relates not just to the edge of creation but to each creature. In its own proper way corresponding to the fidelity of God and suiting itself to all creatures, quality and form are bestowed."[4] How does divine love unfold in intelligent races on other planets? What are modes of supernatural life like? That there are numerous bands on the spectrum of special divine presence in planetary life is likely, because spiritual and graced existence is higher and richer.

PARTICLES, QUANTA, AND FIELDS

The cosmos of galaxies is vast. Moreover, scientists have found another world existing for those on Earth, one that is extraordinarily small. It is composed of very tiny entities, both complex and active. Atoms are not the ultimate building blocks of reality, for they themselves are composed of particles. Different kinds of particles fashion material things. A glass of water or of wine seems static, of a single color, unmoving, while, in fact, in the elements making up the liquid there is a constellation of moving atoms, and within the atoms are particles, billions of them. These particles are much smaller than the nucleus of an atom. Minute subatomic filaments of energy vibrate and produce energies and particles, and the universe of things emerges in the subatomic realm.[5]

In recent years, scientists established an ensemble called The Standard Model aiming to list and describe the fundamental particles in matter like quarks, leptons, and bosons. Some of these elementary particles exist only for fractions of a second. They seem to influence and attract one another at a distance as well as when in contact. The *muon* is one of these fundamental subatomic particles; it is a kind of neutrino. Muons are created in distant atmospheres and constantly hit every inch of the Earth's surface; they pass through almost any substance, not stopping until they penetrate far below the surface of the Earth, more than a mile. Almost without any mass, they never touch another reality. Many trillions of them pass through our bodies each second.

Researchers into subatomic particles have been struck by similarities between a photograph of a tiny subatomic particle crashing into a solid obstacle and a photograph of the immediate aftermath of the Big Bang now seen by telescopes looking far into the past. The exploding patterns of subatomic particles seem to resemble the Big Bang. Do enormous clusters of galaxies and minute atomic particles have similarities? Is a primal explosion like the momentary existence of a neutrino? Are there living entities on other planets that are living on a subatomic scale?

Reflections on the structure of fields may indicate how divine influence offers to persons guidance and inspiration. Joseph Bracken has sought to develop a theology of cosmology and of graced anthropology within fields.[6] A particle seems to be a vibrating wave in a particular field. Electromagnetic and gravitational fields hold and energize photons of light that carry electromagnetism as well as subatomic quarks and neutrinos. The recently discovered and prominent Higgs-boson particle arises from a field pervading all of space. Caleb Scharf concludes, "When we talk about the physics of the sub-atomic we are talking about all the repercussions that come from fields....We're brushing up against the very real limits of human knowledge and the constraints of our instruments of investigation. Fields, waves, and quanta are a part of our quest into the underpinnings of the world."[7] Different particles emerge in different ways at different times from a collection of fields. As human beings are subsystems within their social systems, do social fields and communities vivify their members in original ways on other planets? How does this relate to the foundational fields of the Trinity?

THE SUBATOMIC AND THE SPIRIT'S PRESENCE

For Christian belief and theology, these particles and their forces could suggest ways in which the divine enters into the human personality.[8] Believers affirm that subtle influences come to each person from God's inspiration and guidance. They may find new theological expressions for grace and revelation in the structures of reality that are much smaller than an atom and more elusive than the waves of gravity or light. Fields, quanta, waves, and minute particles show ways for Christian anthropology to pass beyond the format of a superficial mechanics of nature and grace, willpower and actions, so frequent in past theologies.

Human nature has its pursuits and capabilities; the Bible tells us of God's occasional activities in people. For centuries, from Augustine to the baroque era, what was called "nature" and "grace" were generic terms for the human and the divine. Grace has often been conceived as a transient force. There were several kinds: actual and sanctifying, charism and office sustaining, baptismal and matrimonial. Traditional models of nature and grace rarely got beyond a mechanics of divine power moving through the human will or implanting religious ideas and commitments. For theologians like Thomas Aquinas, however, grace is not a passing force from a heavenly power plant but God's love producing a modality of life. Men and women have biological lives and personalities; they have also been given a further life in the Holy Spirit. Grace is not something occasional or spectacular nor invisible and supranatural; it is ordinary, present, and subtle like human life or gravity. A theology of contacts by God can learn from subatomic structures about ways of explaining interaction between the human personality with its willpower and emotions and divine initiatives. How would "justification," "charism," or "predestination" be viewed in light of this particular microworld? Heidi Russell writes, "Quantum physics is teaching us that everything that exists is interconnected and affects everything else that exists. Reality by its very nature is interconnectedness."[9] "Grace" may resemble particles and waves.

The human spirit can be led beyond fixed limits and cosmic locations. The present is the opening of a reality with a past leading into the future.[10] Russell, drawing on quantum theologies of particles, writes,

> All of our potential or possible choices are part of a larger reality that is encompassed by God in the same way that all of the virtual states of microphysical objects are part of a quantum reality that encompasses both potentiality and actuality. In our freedom we actualize some of that potentiality but what we do not actualize continues to exist virtually in God. God contains the whole.[11]

Probability, potentiality, and future events are active in each moment bringing new perspectives on "the kingdom of God" or "the resurrection."

In a world of planets with a cosmic ecumenism, God relates to billions of intelligent and called beings through the interconnectedness of realities. Star clusters and their planets have their own structures—some minute, some planetary, all of them unique. Their inhabitants, wise and loving, receive fields and particles of divine love.

8

PLANETARY AND TRANSFORMATIONAL TIME

The pulse of the universe is time. Time races through galactic systems, forms cultural eras on Earth, and pervades daily human life. Nonetheless, time is not easily understood. Is time a reality? Does time fly? Do we waste time?

Astronomers in Greece saw time as the measure of the motion of objects, namely the stars, while the Christian theologian Augustine in Roman North Africa wondered if time were not a facet of the inner self. A medieval Jewish philosopher wrote, "Time is composed of atoms, that is to say, of numerous parts that cannot be further subdivided on account of their short duration."[1] The modern philosopher Martin Heidegger saw time not as the seconds of a chronometer but as a cultural atmosphere permeating an individual's existence: "Time is not something which is found outside, found somewhere, as a framework for world events. Time is even less something pulsating inside a person's consciousness. It is, rather, that which makes possible the person to be-ahead-of itself and to be already-involved in what is coming."[2] Times bring different cultures. They emerge century after century presenting thought forms that fashion people's lives. Realms ranging from music to biology assume dynamics, color, and organization from a particular culture. For instance, Egyptian and baroque cultures differ in their expression of psychology, music, and religion. Scientists offer theories about time's calculation, while poets and novelists compose narratives about men and women caught up in a dangerous time. Time gets into us, permeates us. We don't have time; time has us.

PLANETS AND TIMES

Explorations of the universe and of the atom have revealed different modes of time. Suns and planets with their speeds and minerals are numerous, and each has its time, its evolution with its periods. There do not seem to be galaxies or subatomic particles without some temporality. Each being is caught up in its own times and in the times around it. Temporalities are being fashioned in the universe right now. Are all these times grounded in a single temporality of depth and length? George Coyne observes that Earth and our societies are evolving within the wide universe. "Why are we drawn ever onward, searching for a comprehensive understanding of it all but never reaching the All? From the intricate patterns of DNA to the magnificent structure of galaxies we are brought to wonder: to wonder about origins, to wonder about ends, to wonder about purpose, and to wonder whether involved in all of this there is a person."[3] Pierre Teilhard de Chardin wrote, "Creation has never stopped. The creative act is one huge, continual gesture, drawn out over the totality of time. It is still going on. Incessantly, even if imperceptively, the world is constantly emerging, each moment a little farther above nothingness."[4] Times, past and future, hold limited aspects of divine initiatives and projects.

A DIVINE GIFT

Being and time are gifts from the beginning, from origins, from the Originator. On Earth, we imagine time and history as a linear arrow from the past going through the present to the future. Karl Rahner observed that "God creates as human time something of his own temporality in order to impart to humanity something of eternity."[5] The richness of God's life encompasses all temporalities: it enables them; it does not stand over against them. Bernard Sesboüé writes, "Divine eternity is so much eternity that it is capable of assuming the reality of time into itself, transcending, while respecting, it at one and the same time. In freely creating the world and, with it, time, God has already put himself in a relationship with time which he embraces as a unity."[6] Times and histories unfold in Christianity. That faith speaks of several kinds of times—of a salvation history or of a mysticism of the present moment. Time is revelatory and calls upon humanity to look beyond terrestrial matters—to accept the potentialities of creation and to contemplate the glory of a future. Future times are not always destructive or empty but can be filled with transforming life. Time is varied, cultural, astrophysical, and sacramental. Persons are aware of several temporalities and of their relationships to other worlds. Time is a channel and forming medium of grace.

OTHER SALVATION HISTORIES

Times empower life and change in the universe. John Haught develops a theology of cosmic evolution that has a long future: "The cosmos seems to be still in its beginning stages. What does an unfinished universe imply for spiritual and ethical lives? At present the flow of time is coupled with growth and decay although in a new creation the flow of time is characterized only by growth and that space-time is real but not limiting in the same way as in this creation."[7] Human history unfolds within time as it meets there a divine presence. Where does the history of salvation on Earth stand in the spectrum of God's many temporal endeavors? One-third of the way through? Toward the end?

Like people on Earth in their expressions of revelation and grace, intelligent beings on other planets would live in temporalities drawn from their worlds. Times influencing one particular world would be different from those of another planet. Jacques Arnould concludes, "With the discovery of other peoples, the horizon of what is past might well yield to the horizon of the future. Creation is not grasped and expressed just as the preservation of a primitive state considered to be perfect but as a work of the future."[8] Cosmologies open onto eschatologies.

Planets are related to other planets. Roger Haight concludes, "Persons are inseparable from a universe composed of events that occur in the present and are thrust into the past; then new possibilities keep arriving from out of the future. The whole cosmic story is received everlastingly into the vivifying immediacy of God's experience. Since everything that happens in our personal lives is woven into the fabric of the whole universe in an unrepeatable way, each person's life is taken along with the whole cosmic story into God."[9] Beyond clocks and atoms, in galaxies and on other planets, touched and empowered by God, there may be several times, ages, and events that are atmospheres of grace in persons. Haight argues, "Why should we suppose that God could transform and reconstitute only human narratives and not just as readily the stories of all living subjects? Any other God would be too small for not only human organism but also the whole evolutionary drama of life."[10] Extraterrestrials in their time, space, and intelligence would have their own frameworks of temporality—galactic, subatomic, psychological, and religious.

TRANSFORMATIONS

Transformations—"eternity," "heaven," "resurrection," "eschaton"—are the results of time. They are stages and realizations in the future. They are gifts from deeper realms, both cosmic and divine. Thomas Aquinas saw transformed life in and beyond human nature as the ordinary future of people on Earth. This view is forecast by the new condition of Jesus of Nazareth being risen. "Resurrection," he noted, "cannot be a principle of nature although resurrection finds its goal in the life of nature."[11] Here, resurrection is a mode of human life. Would not other planetary religions have their transformations? If intelligent civilizations do exist on planets circling stars in the Milky Way, they may have already passed into new self-realizations.

Does human death block transformation or lead to it? Is mortality as powerful and omnipresent in other worlds as it is on planet Earth? Do all intelligent creatures, by virtue of their constitution, move toward death? Other planets may have different forms of life and different forms of "death." Does dying usually or always serve as a portal to forms of life? Are there forms of life that lead to transfigured life without dying? How do intelligent beings in other worlds experience death? Death may be a time of peaceful metamorphosis providing experience and learning. Some theologians offer a positive exploration of death. Death does not simply withdraw a person from the world and make him or her acosmic. It transposes them into a new and more comprehensive relationship to the world. They are freed from the confines of a single place and world, from many limitations of an earthly existence.[12] Death sets the person free to change and to expand.

Music, painting, and literature point to stories of survival and transformation. Beyond death is further life. Early Eastern Christian theology presumed that humanity, all men and women, had been fashioned not for death or the extinction of their race but for further life. Gregory of Nyssa wrote that to be human is to be created for immortality.[13] There comes to human beings a happy fulfillment to people's histories of freedom, of a pervasiveness of the enabling and saving presence of God. This will occur in the universe and not just on the continents of Earth.

Astrophysical discoveries and theological beliefs in an optimism of universal dimensions will temper anxious prophecies such as "the end of the world," "the resurrection of the dead," "the second coming," and "the last judgment." These dramatic events lead to life. After death, everyone enters a further life process directed by God where they meet countless beings of intelligence, love, and creativity. Grace after death personalizes a man or a woman to a high degree.

Transformation draws countless lives into new cultures. In the third century, Clement of Alexandria taught of "the whole of nature surrounding the human person" being transformed.[14] Haught adds that "to be raised bodily from the dead is to experience the constantly new meaning of deeper connectedness to the total cosmos as it is received into God's love....The basis of our resurrection would be God's own relatedness to the world, a relatedness which consists of God's compassionate saving of all events everlastingly in the divine experience."[15] Christians are materialists: they believe that, for those living on Earth, the Holy Spirit brings a qualitatively new bodily life after death. A transfigured body may live out of points and fields of energy, out of particles of matter in act. Joseph Bracken develops the concepts of life and temporality as fields:

Jesus consciously established a new corporate field
of activity which he referred to as the kingdom of
God. Thereby he was adding to the structure of the
already existing divine-human field of activity that
the three divine persons shared with all their creatures as a result of the initial act of creation, the
beginning of the cosmic process.[16]

Both astrophysics and theology refer to time as a field of reality and change—for living.

Is resurrection or transformation exceptional in the universe or ordinary? For Brian Robinette, resurrection is for
matter and for spirit "the grammar," the underlying dynamic
format that enhances an individual.[17] The one individual on
Earth who rose from the dead could be an important affirmation (but not a solitary exemplar) of transformations on
other planets. Scarcely imaginable transformations give further power to planetary people in their futures. Haught concludes, "Both contemporary science and biblical hope view
the universe as open to dramatic transformation....Cosmologi-
cal, geological, and biological accounts of cosmic events teach
us that nature has always had a dramatic character."[18] What
do planetary persons become through their specific transformations? Do they have histories? Perhaps a few or many
intelligent societies are vitalized through one or more transfigurations. Regardless, inhabitants of planets move beyond
their first planetary modes of existence in striking ways.

The cosmos is a gathering empowered by many temporalities and moving toward an unknown but colorful future.
The patterns of evolution in beings suggest that such developments would be widespread in the galaxies. The end of
our observable universe is not universal termination but a
variety of further stages in the realization of God's creativity.
Heidi Russell states, "Our eternal significance consists in being

part of the evolution of something bigger than ourselves.... Our great hope in God can be that we are not the end of the story of creation, that creation continues after the extinction of humanity, after the death of our sun and solar system."[19] Terrestrial resurrection and transformation—realizations of a special field of energy—are part of a Earth's ecology of time. St. Paul's observation, "For here we have no lasting city, but we are looking for the city that is to come" (Heb 13:14), takes on cosmic applications. There is "a pancosmicity" of the personal and the graced. Haught concludes, "Human beings are at last witnessing what may turn out to be a distinctively new explosion in the unfolding of our far-from-finished universe. Theology must approach the specter of transhumanism with the reverence of the sacramental vision."[20] Transformation will happen in a particular way to individuals, to civilizations, and to the entire cosmos. Plans are at work in countless worlds.

9

VISITORS TO EARTH FROM OTHER WORLDS

Extraterrestrials are intelligent, corporeal beings living on planets orbiting suns that are far away from Earth. The great number of stars and exoplanets being discovered suggests that there are many forms of animal and vegetable life in the universe. Some of these are probably persons of matter and body with minds and freedom. How many intelligent civilizations were living in the universe four billion years ago? How many societies are yet to come in the hundreds of millions of years ahead?

ALIENS AND RELIGIONS

For centuries, astronomers as well as novelists have imagined contact with other worlds. Those encounters with intelligent beings emerged first as the fictional journeys of humans to the moon, or to Venus or Mars. In the late second century CE, Lucian of Samosata, a native of Syria who moved to Athens, wrote several novels and satirical works that mocked schools of philosophy as well as Christianity. In one novel, he described a visit to the moon and to Venus where their inhabitants were encountered. There are wars between the citizens of the sun and those of the moon. His novel may be the earliest work of science fiction.

Around that same time, as we have noted, some theologians, living in Hellenistic cultural circles two centuries after the emergence of the Christian faith, held theories about intelligent beings in the cosmos. One of these, Origen, thought that some stars visible in the sky are themselves alive and knowing. Alan Scott concluded, "Like all his contemporaries, Origen thinks that the universe was filled with rational, spiritual beings who had powers and responsibilities which were much greater than those of the human race. Like his predecessors in Hellenistic philosophy, he divides these beings into angels and heavenly bodies without making clear how these two groups were related to each other."[1] Astronomers, novelists, poets, and philosophers have had ideas for centuries about other races of intelligence inhabiting planets and stars.

Religions speak of angels, demigods, seraphim, and so on. Carl Sagan wrote, "Our language has no really appropriate terms for such beings."[2] Some religions picture intermediary creatures between an ultimate God and people on Earth. These may be gathered in a pantheon of active deities (as with Apollo obeying Zeus), or they could be quasi-divine forces, demiurges, who assist God in creation. Some religious directions like those of the Persians elaborated theories about angelic beings, who are creatures without matter. A pattern of a royal court around God is suggested by the few early Jewish references to spiritual powers; moreover, in Hebrew the *el* at the end of the names of angels (e.g., "Gabriel," "Raphael") indicates a Semitic linguistic reference to God, *El*, and so it is possible that angels were seen as extensions of divine activity. At the time of Jesus and afterward, Judaism, influenced by other religions, speculated on different kinds of angels sent by God to instruct or assist chosen men and women.[3] For the readers of the Bible, however, if God has messengers, there is no cult directed toward them.

For Thomas Aquinas, an angel is a being physically and metaphysically in an intermediate stage between the single absolute divinity and material creatures. Each angel is a distinct "species": its solely spiritual nature, its specific knowledge, and its mobility come from the specific natural form of this spiritual being. Over time, people on Earth have wondered whether these manifestations are totally spiritual or slightly material. And what are their capabilities—rapid travel, playing the harp? An angel is not an "extraterrestrial." In recent years, some have proposed that God employed extraterrestrials from other planets and solar systems to be what Earth interpreted as his messengers. This, however, remains unknown. We learn nothing about extraterrestrials—about their being, natures, and cosmic locations—from the Bible.

When the knowledge arrives that intelligent extraterrestrials exist, this will challenge and expand religious perspectives on what have been called "angels." Such purely spiritual, little-known beings can exist. Material and intellectual persons on other planets might affirm too that there are other intermediate beings—not Earthlings and not angels—in the cosmos. If planets are numerous, their inhabitants will be numerous and varied. The relationships of Earth to spheres of beings and to the Ultimate would be remarkable and scarcely imaginable. Initially, the role of angels, past and present, would be uncertain.

THE CHALLENGES OF TIME AND SPACE

Much of the Milky Way, Earth's stellar region, might be presumed to be sterile. In fact, Earth and other worlds are islands in interstellar realms that are largely empty.[4] The stars in the cosmos in stellar clusters and galaxies are occupying only between 4 and 8 percent of the volume of space in the universe. Interspersed among these clusters of stars or galaxies are immense empty spaces where only a few, if any, burning suns exist. Most of the volume of the plane encompassing the galaxies is a great quasi-void.

There are challenges to any contact with an extraterrestrial species.[5] Two gulfs separate Earth from the planets elsewhere in the Milky Way and from planets in further galaxies: time and space.

The evolution of the cosmos has its own times, often staggeringly lengthy. The odds are not high that other civilizations present in the cosmos will overlap in time with terrestrial science. An encounter with another civilization needs an intersection when the temporal cycles of technologies in other worlds coincide with advances on Earth. Some civilizations on planets lie hundreds of millions of years in the past; others will reach scientific maturity millions of years in the future. Hundreds of millions of years pass in the production of suns and planets, and of their life-forms including intelligent cultures. Each society of intelligence and technology probably endures for a period of two hundred thousand years to two million years. The absence of indications of intelligent life elsewhere in the universe may not necessarily mean that intelligent civilizations have not existed there but that those cultures, too, have passed through their limited lifetimes. Earth may miss the flourishing of other cosmic civilizations in their technologically advanced periods. To look ahead to many habitable and scientifically advanced planets is to look forward to planets yet to be formed. An intelligent species that learns how to determine the ages of stars and galaxies will come to these sobering conclusions about the intersection of worlds existing in ages far apart.

The second gulf or barrier is distance. Intelligent civilizations might be somewhat rare in a particular galaxy, and rare in our galaxy. Our immediate surroundings in the Milky Way are sparsely populated. In our region, the separation between neighboring star systems is four or five light years. The closest star to Earth and the sun is Proxima Centauri, four-and-a-quarter light-years away, or about twenty-five trillion miles. Even with greatly advanced, accelerated means of travel, the time to reach the closest stellar neighbor is estimated to be between 60,000 and 110,000 years.[6]

LISTENING FOR OTHERS

For centuries, some scientists, philosophers, and religious leaders have insisted that beings from other worlds have come close to planet Earth. This is an uncertainty: no clear evidence of even one brief visit survives scrutiny.

Over the last twenty years, the chances have improved for contact because of the discovery of exoplanets. Twenty percent (or more) of those planets being discovered are in a habitable zone, a location in relation to their sun that is conducive to life and has similarities to the situation of Earth. Searches for extraterrestrial intelligence in other galaxies is beginning. As already noted, the psychologist and historian of science Douglas Vakoch has been active in looking for signals from advanced civilizations. He examines solar regions from which contacts, or responses, might come to Earth. Signals are sent repeatedly for a time to a particular celestial object. Here, distance also offers challenges. What are the most effective media for sending and phrasing messages within the context of the evolution of intelligence and language? SETI seeks to contact planets around stars through mathematical or chemical formulae sent out repeatedly; it looks for pulses coming back from civilizations. This activity faces the challenge of various languages, technologies, and thought forms employed within the cosmos.[7] Vakoch summarizes, "Signals will have traversed trillions of miles, reaching Earth after traveling for years. Using a more sober estimate of the prevalence of life in the universe, our closest interstellar interlocutors may be so remote from Earth that their signals would take centuries or millennia to reach us."[8]

Connected to space and time is the challenge of evolutionary divergence. Extraterrestrials and Earthlings have had independent biological evolutions and independent cultural histories:

> Any civilization we contact will have arisen independently of life on Earth, in the habitable zone of a star stable enough to allow its inhabitants to evolve biologically, culturally, and technologically. The evolutionary path followed by extraterrestrial intelligence will no doubt diverge in significant ways from the one traveled by humans over the course of our history.[9]

How much will one planet understand from another? Their religions, part of their cultural realms, will have aspects of originality.

Scientists hold that contact with extraterrestrials is in its early stages. Michio Kaku concludes,

> It is safe to say that within this century it would be strange if we did not detect signals from another civilization in space....Direct conversations between them and us would be difficult, given their enormous distance from us. First it may take months to years to decode fully the message, and then to rank this civilization's technology. Second direct communication with them will probably be unlikely

since the distance to this civilization will be many light years away, too far for any direct contact.[10]

Contact may mean slight electronic signals, awareness rather than conversation. Planets might not expend much effort to contact other civilizations.

ASTRAL VISITORS: VIOLENT OR SYMPATHETIC?

Science fiction often presents extragalactic planetary civilizations as hostile and destructive.[11] Thus violence pervades the universe. As we noted, in journals on astrophysics—popular or academic—atoms and stars contact each other in descriptive ways implying fiery destruction, invasions, or annihilation. What, in fact, is being described, however, are the ordinary processes of nature; the universe's evolutions are the unfolding of matter and forces. Pursuing a different direction, some presume that efforts to communicate with other worlds will meet only silence because technologically advanced societies would have inevitably destroyed themselves.[12] This is pessimism on a cosmic scale. The history of sin and salvation recorded in the two testaments of the Bible is a particular religious history on one planet and not the single framework for all civilizations. Religion is not necessarily mainly about suffering although it is such for some groups on Earth. Terrestrial religions should not assert claims about races on other planets and their situation amid grace and sin. Haught writes, "Cosmic hope rejects cosmic pessimism because the latter makes a morbid settlement with the realm of death by cultivating a metaphysics that absolutizes the fixed and lifeless past."[13] Extraterrestrials could be our teachers and mentors, our friends and coworkers, supportive and sympathetic.

The Christian perspective gives a positive view of the future of the cosmos. The resurrection of individuals is part of a cosmic drama of transformation, beauty, and life. In the universe of the future, and probably even now, billions of individuals pass through space, transformed, to visit welcoming worlds.

10

LIVING IN AN INTRAGALACTIC SOCIETY

The cosmos is a city of suns. Today, its billions of fiery orbs are implying other worlds, exoplanets, to us on Earth. Not only science but faith and theology can learn from this universe. The kingdom of God's openness to all peoples on Earth and science's exploration of planets' identities both lead to a cosmic ecumenism.

A SKY OF STARS

Millions of stars surround the Earth. Humans can see only a few thousand of them, although light from countless others is streaming toward this planet. Exoplanets come in a variety of sizes: some orbit multiple stars systems; some stay close to their parental suns; others are distant. If only one out of every 150,000 exoplanets in the universe contain life, there would be a million worlds with life in an average galaxy like the Milky Way. Each will have its animals, flowers, and flying carnivores. What percentage of planets with life forms hold intelligent life?

As we have noted, there is not only a large universe of galaxies but a minute one of subatomic particles that exist for fractions of a second—very small particles, brought together by forces of gravity, electricity, magnetism, light, and speed, form a planet's realities. That almost invisible realm could also suggest the variety of ways by which the divine fashions and contacts beings.

Like a theme arising from a large orchestra in a constant crescendo, the cosmos resounds with the motif of *more*. Earth, now and in the future, is located among galaxies and planets that likely hold societies and communities.

LIVING AMONG THE EXOPLANETS

Exoplanets are extra-planets. More planets suggest more companions for Earth. Two scientists, Nancy Abrams and Joel Primack, observe that "the new scientific picture is different from all earlier creation stories not only because it is based on evidence but also because it is the first picture created by collaboration among people from different religions, races, and cultures from around the world. The new universe picture excludes no one and sees all as equals."[1] In other galaxies, far away planets may be home to creatures of intelligence who under the light of bright moons fashion imaginative science and music. They note, "To explore and gradually move out into the Galaxy is a project that could be successfully undertaken only by a long-lived civilization with a shared, unifying cosmology that accurately reflects the universe....To be able to achieve this, the society would have to be a cosmic society, understanding our central place in the universe and the value of intelligence to the evolution of the whole."[2] Other planetary cultures, researching other worlds, will also be challenged because of the intellectual powers and kinds of perceptions that are natural to people on quite diverse planets. Nonetheless, they may engage the future more accurately than human intelligence, and perhaps their grasp of and mastery over velocities are greater. Regardless, the future holds an expanding dialogue beyond Earth and its solar system.

For human beings, life on Earth leads to further life: resurrection in a transformed world. Transfigured persons will explore exoplanets where they meet the lives of others and can visit civilizations advanced in science, psychology, and art.

The universe is one. Exoplanets suggest that space and time can bring numerous contacts with others to each society. There could be federations of galaxies where vast amounts of information are held collectively.[3] John Haught notes this bond of all beings:

> All galaxies (and even all universes, if others exist) are rooted in an ultimate unity of being; so travels from Earth could never bring us into an encounter with anything completely alien to us. Theology's relevance to the breadth of cosmos lies in its conviction that all possible worlds have a common origin and depth in the one God. And by virtue of the omnipresence of the one God, we too would have an extended home in other possible worlds.[4]

The identity of each person on Earth would deepen through relationships with other planets. Individuals are connected to other corporeal intelligences who exist, have existed, and will exist. Furthermore, personal identity may be intertwined with the lives of those who live much later.[5]

These pages can bring an uneasiness with terms like *extraterrestrials*. The deeper shock, however, is not that a strange-looking race of intelligent creatures might exist somewhere. What is startling is that there would seem to be so many populations of intelligence on planets orbiting many suns. They do not all exist now. Some have come and gone, fading away into God's providence hundreds of millions of years ago. Others will flourish far in the future. James Gardner notes,

> Life and intelligence are at the center of the vast, seemingly impersonal physical processes of the universe. Some scientists see the inhabited cosmos as a kind of ecosystem-in-waiting—a universe custom-made for the purpose of yielding life and ever-ascending intelligence. It follows that every creature and every intelligent entity—great and small, biological and post-biological—plays an indefinable some role in an awesome process by which intelligence gains hegemony over inanimate nature.[6]

All this challenges our human faiths to believe that a person is significant even in this ocean of stars. There is a divine knowledge of and love for me, a dignity for the existence of each individual in societies small or large.

Intelligence fashions cultures in times and civilizations. Mark Lupisella introduces a dialogue between cosmos and culture:

> Culture having importance for the universe might be called "Cosmocultural Evolution," or the "Cosmocultural Principle"; it suggests that perhaps a sufficiently different kind of evolution is emerging—the co-evolution of cosmos and culture, where culture plays an important and perhaps critical role. Strong versions of cosmocultural evolution could be interpreted to suggest that cultural evolution is in some sense "on par" with physical cosmic evolution...and has unlimited potential.[7]

Astrotheology ponders how both personal intelligence and divine presence are active over millions of years and on millions of planets.

Eight centuries ago, Thomas Aquinas preached a sermon on how happiness beyond death includes living in a society. Its members would be God and angels and human beings—all the intelligent beings he knew.[8] He described future life as learning and traveling. The risen human being has a special gift of *agilitas* that makes the movements of the corporeal person subject at once to the ideas and intentions of its mental, animating principle. The risen body moves "subject to the glorified soul in the most powerful way, smoothly obeying the impulses of the will."[9] Sciences and arts will draw planetary inhabitants into the wider universe. "After they have ascended upwards into the heavens, it is likely that they will at times move, move just as it pleases them. By putting into action what lies in their own power, they show forth the greatness of divine wisdom. Their vision is refreshed by the beauty of the variety of creatures in which God's wisdom shines forth in the highest way."[10] The universe's complexity and divine presences entertain and educate. They understand what they visit in a cosmic tourism.

COSMIC FAITHS AND RELIGIONS

Galaxies expanding into space may hold planets full of persons with their spiritualities, liturgies, and space ethics.[11] The inhabitants of unusual planets with forests of purple and silver in the light of ten moons wonder about the Source of all that they see. They think about transcendence, love, the future, and transformation. They experience awe and reverence, faith and hope. On this or that exoplanet, there are liturgies and mystical experiences: a bird may have no symbolic meaning; blood may be unknown; other forms might assume the role of water. Information, sciences, and unifying theories from these further societies would offer themes and thought forms for theology. Through further incarnations, they tell of their intelligent species and of the Trinity.

Faith attains a cosmic dimension as billions of distinctive persons explore the divine presence. Thomas Berry writes,

> Just as Christianity in its developing phase established itself in intimate relations with the structure and functioning of the world in its liturgical processes, so now there is a need to adopt a new sense of a self-emergent universe as a sacred mode whereby the divine becomes present to the human community....Revelation, incarnation, and redemption are primarily for the entire universe, not primarily for any group of individual beings within the universe.[12]

Cosmic religious communities will not so much fashion dogmas in unusual languages or celebrating rites imitating cycles of a particular moon but disclose new contacts with the divine. For the intelligent person, there would be star mentors: astronomers and astrophysicists, mathematicians and astrobiologists, experts in technology and novelists, and stellar photographers and theologians. They assist each other in conversations between science and faith.[13]

COMMUNITIES AND GALAXIES

A risen individual is a citizen of a world of worlds.[14] The procession of those dying on their planet does not enter an empty paradise. Peter Phan writes, "The resurrection of the dead not only concerns the reunion of my soul with my body but also the social reunion of myself and the other members of the Body of Christ, particularly my family and friends."[15] The transformed of Earth meet the citizens of other planets. The Trinity sends out personal and social vitalizations to planets in ways suited to their cultures. Civilizations become present to and assist one other. The vast universe—its families and nations—gives a galactic realization to a theme of St. Paul: "we, who are many, are one body in Christ, and individually we are members one of another" (Rom 12:5).

Faith is not mainly an acceptance of some rare and miraculous events in the past. It is the affirmation of a future unfolding divine plans in varied forms of life. John Haught focuses his cosmic theology forward. God is not a governing judge but an attracting goal; life and society are less a structure than a drama; the cosmic narrative is luminous and eschatological.[16] He notes, "Any distinctively Christian theology must think of God as having the breadth and depth of feeling to take into the divine life the entire cosmic story....Within the embrace of a self-humbling God, the whole universe and its finite history can be transformed into an everlasting beauty."[17] The cosmos holds countless realms of beings, solar systems, and persons; it enables billions of persons to contribute to the ongoing formation of the universe.

Each of the previous chapters points in its own way to the planetary, the personal, the scientific, and the divine. The theme of this book is the Earth's future theological issues: the structures of the universe; the diversity and extent of intelligence; the various kinds of divine assistance; the value of the individual; personal transfigurations; incarnations; and the characteristics of future planetary companions. The universe is born of profound intelligence and continues through expansive love. The divine is a gifted planner.

NOTES

INTRODUCTION

1. George V. Coyne, SJ, and Alessandro Omizzolo, *Wayfarers In The Cosmos: The Human Quest for Meaning* (New York: Crossroad Publishing, 2002), 11.

2. Jo Marchant, *The Human Cosmos: Civilization and the Stars* (New York: Penguin Random House, 2020), 6.

3. Joseph A. Bracken, *Reciprocal Causality in an Event-Filled World* (New York: Fortress Academic, 2022), 130; see also Guy Consolmagno (and Paul Mueller), *Would You Baptize an Extraterrestrial? ...and Other Questions from the Astronomers' In-Box at the Vatican Observatory* (New York: Image, 2014).

4. John F. Haught, *The New Cosmic Story: Inside our Awakening Universe* (New Haven, CT: Yale University Press, 2017), 102; see also Haught, "Science, God, and Cosmic Purpose," in *The Cambridge Companion to Science and Religion*, ed. Peter Harrison (Cambridge: Cambridge University Press, 2010), 276–78.

5. See John F. Haught, *Science and Faith: A New Introduction* (Mahwah, NJ: Paulist Press, 2012), 4–19.

6. William Stoeger, "Astrobiology and Beyond: From Science to Philosophy and Ethics," in *Encountering Life in the Universe: Ethical Foundations and Social Implications of Astrobiology*, ed. Chris Impey, Anna H. Spitz, and William Stoeger (Tucson: The University of Arizona Press, 2013), 67–68.

7. Ted Peters, "Astrobiology and Astrochristology," *Zygon* 51, no. 2 (2016): 481; see also Peters, "Astrotheology," in *The Routledge*

Companion to Modern Christian Thought, ed. Chad Meister and James Beilby (London: Routledge, 2013), 838–53.

8. Haught, *The New Cosmic Story*, 3. Some pioneers in astrotheology are Ted Peters, Guy Consolmagno, Heidi Russell, William Stoeger, Armin Kreiner, Jacques Arnould, John Haught, Diarmuid O'Murchu, David Weintraub, and Douglas Vakoch.

9. George V. Coyne, foreword to *Quantum Shift: Theological and Pastoral Implications of Contemporary Developments in Science*, by Heidi Ann Russell (Collegeville, MN: Liturgical Press, 2015), x.

10. David S. Toolan, "Praying in a Post-Einsteinian Universe," *CrossCurrents* 46, no.4 (Winter 1996/97): 437–70.

11. See John F. Haught, "Chaos, Complexity, and Theology," in *Teilhard in the 21st Century*, ed. Arthur Fable and Donald St. John (Maryknoll, NY: Orbis, 2003), 189.

12. Jacques Arnould, *Turbulences dans l'univers: Dieu, les extraterrestres et nous* (Paris: Albin Michel, 2017), 145–46; Jacques Arnould holds a position for ethics and religion at the Centre National d' Études Spatiales in Paris, France; see his publications in French and English.

13. Arnould, *Turbulences dans l'univers*, ix.

CHAPTER 1

1. Brian Greene, *The Fabric of the Cosmos: Space, Time, and the Texture of Reality* (New York: Random House, 2004), 249.

2. Frank Close, Michael Marten, and Christine Sutton, *The Particle Odyssey: A Journey to the Heart of Matter* (Oxford: Oxford University Press, 2004), 187.

3. Greene, *The Fabric of the Cosmos*, 219–20. In 1927, the Belgian priest and physicist Georges Lemaître had first proposed a theory that the expanding universe (then being observed by more powerful telescopes) could have originated through some kind of primordial explosion. His theory was unpopular among scientists: its implications of a beginning, a powerful cause, and an unfolding plan had a religious overtone.

4. Joseph Bracken, *Reciprocal Causality in an Event-Filled World* (Lanham, MD: Fortress Academic, 2022), 79.

Notes

5. Nicolas Cheetham, *Universe: A Journey from Earth to the Edge of the Cosmos* (London: Smith-Davies, 2005), 6–7. On light in science and theology see Gerald O'Collins & Mary Ann Meyers, *Light from Light: Scientists and Theologians in Dialogue* (Grand Rapids, MI: Eerdmans 2012).

6. Serge Brunier, *The Great Atlas of the Stars* (Buffalo, NY: Firefly, 2001), 96–98; see C. J. Conselice, "Our Trillion-Galaxy Universe," *Astronomy* 45, no. 6 (2017): 19–23.

7. Caleb Scharf, *The Zoomable Universe* (New York: Farrar, Strauss, Giroux, 2017), 46.

8. C. Robert O'Dell, *The Orion Nebula: Where Stars Are Born* (Cambridge, MA: Harvard University Press, 2003), 154.

9. Chet Raymo, *Soul of the Night* (Cambridge, MA: Cowley, 2005), 84; see also David Koerner, *Here Be Dragons: The Scientific Quest for Extraterrestrial Life* (Oxford: Oxford University Press, 2000).

10. See Nancy Ellen Abrams and Joel R. Primack, "We Are Stardust," in *The New Universe and the Human Future* (New Haven, CT: Yale University Press, 2011), 39–66.

11. Aquinas, *Summa contra Gentiles* II, 81.

12. George Coyne and Alessandro Omizzolo, *Wayfarers in the Cosmos: The Human Quest for Meaning* (New York: Crossroad Publishing, 2002), 157; see also "Creazione e creatività," *Aquinas* 61, nos. 1–2 (2018).

13. William R. Stoeger, "Describing God's Action in Light of Scientific Knowledge of Reality," in *Chaos and Complexity: Scientific Perspectives on Divine Action*, ed. Robert John Russell et al. (Vatican State: The Vatican Observatory, 2000), 260.

14. Aquinas, *Summa Theologiae* (*ST*) I, q. 91, a. 3.

15. Jacques Arnould, "Introduction. Has the Sky Opened?" in *Space Exploration and ET: Who Goes There?* (Adelaide: ATF, 2014), ix; see Armin Kreiner, *Jesus, UFOs, Aliens: Außerirdische Intelligenz als Herausforderung für den christlichen Glauben* (Freiburg: Herder, 2011), 166.

16. John F. Haught, "Theology after Contact. Religion and Extraterrestrial Intelligent Life," *Annals of the New York Academy of Sciences* 950 (2006): 296–308; see Knut-Willy Saether, "Aesthetics at

the Intersection of Science and Theology," in *Our Common Cosmos: Exploring the Future of Theology, Human Culture and Space Sciences*, ed. Z. L. Imfeld and A. Losch (London: T&T Clark, 2019), 109–24.

17. Are there distinct multiverses? There is no empirical indication of such; no one has detected any trace of another universe. A related question would be, Have there been several big bangs? At present, this is imagination speculating; see Heidi Ann Russell, "The Possibility of a Multiverse," in *Quantum Shift: Theological and Pastoral Implications of Contemporary Developments in Science* (Collegeville, MN: Liturgical Press, 2015), 130–48; J. E. Hafner and J. Valentin, eds., *Parallelwelten: Christliche Religion und die Verfielfachung von Wirklichkeit* (Stuttgart: Kohlhammer, 2009). A careful look at the idea of the multiverse is in Haught, *The New Cosmic Story: Inside our Awakening Universe* (New Haven CT: Yale University Press, 2017), 137–39.

18. Russell, *Quantum Shift*, 107.

CHAPTER 2

1. Aquinas, *Summa Theologiae* (*ST*) I, q. 2, a. 2, ad 3; he wrote, "We" cannot know what God is but only what he is not (ST I, q. 3, Prologue).

2. See John F. Haught, "Spirituality: From Contemplation to Anticipation," in *Resting on the Future: Catholic Theology for an Unfinished Universe* (New York: Bloomsbury, 2015), 43–54.

3. See M. Baumgartner, "Die Philosophie Alanus de Insulis," *Beiträge zur Geschichte der Philosophie des Mittelalters* 2 (1896): 125–39.

4. Aquinas, *ST* I, q. 13, a. 11. Aquinas cited this phrase from a writing of John Damascene in the seventh century (*De Fide Orthodoxa* 29 [Migne, *Patrologia Graeca* 94, 836]).

5. Aquinas, *ST* I, q. 18, a. 3.

6. Aquinas, *Super Evangelium Ioannis Lectura* (1:4) (Turin: Marietti, 1952) ch. 1, lect. 3, 20; see *ST* III, q. 1, a. 1.

7. Aquinas, *ST* I, q. 44, a. 3.

8. Aquinas, *Compendium theologiae ad Fratrem Reginaldum*, c. 9, *Opuscula theologica* 1 (Turin: Marietti, 1953), 133.

9. Werner Eizinger, *Dreifaltigkeit – ein ewiges Mysterium? Den Gott der Christen verstehen* (Regensburg: Pustet, 2013), 93.

10. Aquinas, *ST* I-II, q. 112, a. 1.

11. Karl Rahner, "On the Theology of the Incarnation," in *Theological Investigations* 4 (Baltimore: Helicon, 1966), 113.

12. Aquinas, *ST*, I, q. 22, a. 3.

13. Aquinas, *De Veritate*, q. 23, a. 5.

14. Aquinas, *Summa contra Gentiles* III, 70.

15. Aquinas, *De Veritate*, q. 23, a. 5.

16. William Stoeger, "Cosmology, Evolution, Causality and Creation: The Limits, Compatibility and Cooperation of Scientific and Philosophical Methodologies," in *The Causal Universe*, ed. George F. R. Ellis, Michael Heller, and Tadeusz Pabjan (Cracow: Copernicus Center Press, 2013), 247; see also Christoph Böttinger, *Wie handelt Gott in der Welt? Reflexionen im Spannungsfeld von Theologie und Naturwissenschaft* (Freiburg: Herder, 2013).

17. William Stoeger cited in Stephen Pope, "Does Evolution Have a Purpose? The Theological Significance of William Stoeger's Account of 'Nested Directionality,'" *Theological Studies* 78 (2017): 464.

18. John F. Haught, "Chaos, Complexity, and Theology," in *Teilhard in the 21st Century: The Emerging Spirit of Earth*, ed. Arthur Fabel and Donald St. John (Maryknoll, NY: Orbis Books, 2003), 185.

CHAPTER 3

1. Govert Schilling, "Astronomers Spot Galaxies Clustering in Early Universe," *Sky & Telescope*, May 2021, 10.

2. Arwen Rimmer, "The Very Hungry Universe," *Astronomy* 50, No. 6 (2022): 16–17.

3. Aquinas, *Summa Theologiae (ST)* I, q. 13, a. 11.

4. See Christoph Bruns, *Trinität und Kosmos: Zur Gotteslehre des Origenes* (Münster: Aschendorf, 2013).

5. See Schelling, *System of Transcendental Idealism* (Charlottesville: University Press of Virginia, 1998). "Furthermore, the total evolution of the absolute synthesis is also an infinite process, and history itself is a never wholly completed revelation of that Absolute"

(211); see Emilio Brito, *La Création selon Schelling. Universum* (Leuven: University Press, 1987), 419–20; Walter Kasper, *The Absolute in History: The Philosophy and Theology of History in Schelling's Late Philosophy* (Mahwah, NJ: Paulist Press, 2018).

6. Marc Maeschalk, *Philosophie et révélation dans l'itinéraire de Schelling* (Paris: Vrin, 1989), 521. "In the areas explained by theologians, contemporary research has moved in a direction anticipated by the great thinkers of idealist philosophy during the nineteenth century. In Schelling's system, Trinity and creation are organically and dynamically joined to each other."

7. Greshake, *Der dreieine Gott. Eine trinitarische Theologie* (Freiburg: Herder, 1997), 179.

8. The psychologist C. G. Jung considers the interplay between a triad and the presentation of the ultimate deity on Earth in "A Psychological Approach to the Dogma of the Trinity," *Collected Works XI: Psychology and Religion: West and East* (Princeton, NJ: Princeton University Press, 1969), 109–200.

9. Boff, *Holy Trinity, Perfect Community* (Maryknoll, NY: Orbis, 2000), 3; see Greshake, *Der dreieine Gott*, 32–39; "Trinity as 'Communio,'" in *Rethinking Trinitarian Theology: Disputed Questions and Contemporary Issues in Trinitarian Theology*, ed. Robert J. Wozniak and Giulio Maspero (London: T&T Clark, 2012), 337.

10. Heidi Russell, *The Source of All Love: Catholicity and the Trinity* (Maryknoll, NY: Orbis, 2017), 32.

11. Greshake, *Der dreieine Gott*, 248. Theologians like Greshake and Jürgen Moltmann draw trinitarian theology into "the communicality of creation" (248–52).

12. See Leon Lederman, Beyond the God Particle (Amherst: Prometheus, 2013), 243–44.

13. Joseph A. Bracken, "Panentheism: A Field-Oriented Approach," in *In Whom We Live and Move and Have Our Being: Panentheistic Reflections on God's Presence in a Scientific World*, ed. Philip Clayton and A. R. Peacocke (Grand Rapids, MI: Eerdmans, 2004), 58, 144, 217.

14. Joseph A. Bracken, *The World in the Trinity. Open-Ended Systems in Science and Religion* (Minneapolis: Fortress, 2014), 142. See *Does God Roll Dice? Divine Providence for a World in the Making*

(Collegeville, MN: Liturgical Press, 2012), 82-90, 143-44; T*he One in the Many: A Contemporary Reconstruction of the God-World Relationship* (Grand Rapids, MI: Eerdmans, 2001), 215–17; *God: Three Who Are One* (Collegeville, MN: Liturgical, 2008); see Marc A. Pugliese, *The One, the Many, and the Trinity: Joseph A. Bracken and the Challenge of Process Metaphysics* (Washington, DC: Catholic University of America, 2011).

15. Russell, *The Source of All Love,* 32.

CHAPTER 4

1. Caleb Scharf, *The Zoomable Universe* (New York: Farrar, Strauss, and Giroux, 2017), 73. In France the Institut pour l'Astrophysique de Paris offered the hypothesis that there are more planets than suns in a galaxy, in each galaxy. In our Milky Way there would be eight hundred billion planets for around two hundred billion stars (Guillaume Ducrot, "Les Exoplanètes les plus spectaculaires de 2013," in *Collection Science & Espace: Exoplanètes, les nouveaux mondes* [Nanterre: Éditions Diverti, 2014], 29–39). Natalie Batalha, Kepler mission scientist at NASA's Ames Research Center in California, said calculations suggest that there could be more than ten billion potentially habitable planets in the Milky Way. "Nearest habitable planet 'close' says Nasa" (https://inews.co.uk/news/science/nasa-says-nearest-habitable-planet-probably-11-light-years-away-6543, May 11, 2016).

2. Alan Boss, *The Crowded Universe: The Race to Find Life beyond Earth* (New York: Basic Books, 2009), 205; see the early work of Isaac Asimov, *Extra-terrestrial Civilizations* (New York: Crown Publications, 1979).

3. John F. Haught, *The New Cosmic Story: Inside our Awakening Universe* (New Haven, CT: Yale University Press, 2017), 44–45.

4. Aquinas, *Summa Theologiae* (*ST*) I, q. 75, a. 4.

5. Timothy Ferris, "Worlds Apart," *National Geographic*, December, 2009, 93; see Donald Goldsmith, *Exoplanets: Hidden Worlds and the Quest for Extraterrestrial Life* (Cambridge, MA: Harvard University Press, 2018), chapter 10.

6. Nancy Ellen Abrams and Joel Primack, *The New Universe and the Human Future* (New Haven, CT: Yale University Press, 2011), 162–63.

7. Aquinas, *ST* II-II, q. 8, a. 1, ad 1 & 2.

8. Karl Rahner, "Christology within an Evolutionary View," *Theological Investigations* 5 (Baltimore: Helicon, 1966), 173.

9. See William Stoeger, "Astrobiology and Beyond: From Science to Philosophy and Ethics," in *Encountering Life in the Universe*, ed. C. Impey et al. (Tucson: University of Arizona Press, 2013), 69–79.

10. Surveying the history of exploring ETs prior to SETI, see Douglas Vakoch and Albert Harrison, eds., *Civilizations beyond Earth: Extraterrestrial Life and Society* (New York: Bergmann Books, 2011), 1–28.

11. Jacques Arnould, *Turbulences en l'univers. Dieu, les extraterrestres et nous* (Paris: Albin Michel, 2017), 16; see this work for a detailed history of terrestrial considerations of other beings.

12. Paul Wason, "Inferring Intelligence: Prehistoric and Extra-terrestrial," in *Archaeology, Anthropology, and Interstellar Communication*, ed. Douglas Vakoch (Washington, DC: NASA, 2014), 129; Paul Davies, "Weird Extremophiles," in *The Eerie Silence: Renewing Our Search for Alien Intelligence* (Boston: Houghton Miflin Harcourt, 2010), 47–51.

13. Carl Sagan, *The Varieties of Scientific Experience: A Personal View of the Search for God* (New York: The Penguin Press, 2006), 112.

14. Christiaan Huygens, *The Celestial Worlds Discover'd: Or, Conjectures Concerning the Inhabitants, Plants, and Productions of the Worlds in the Planets* (London: Frank Cass, 1968), 74; see Douglas Vakoch, "The Evolution of Extraterrestrials: The Evolutionary Synthesis and Estimate of the Prevalence of Intelligence beyond Earth," in *Archaeology, Anthropology, and Interstellar Communication*, chapter 12.

15. Jo Marchant, *The Human Cosmos: Civilization and the Stars* (New York: Dutton, 2020), 277; see Jill C. Tarter, "Exoplanets, Extremophiles, and the Search for Extraterrestrial Intelligence," in *Communication with Extraterrestrial Intelligence*, ed. Douglas Vakoch (Albany: SUNY Press, 2011), 5–22; Christian de Duve, *Life Evolving: Molecules, Mind, and Meaning* (Oxford: Oxford University Press,

2002); "Astrobiology," in *Astronomica* ed. Fred Watson (Elanora Heights, Australia: Millennium House, 2007), 160–63.

16. John F. Haught, *Science and Faith: A New Introduction* (Mahwah, NJ: Paulist Press, 2013), 169–176.

17. Haught, *Science and Faith*, 176.

18. Bob Berman, "Alien Life," *Astronomy*, November, 2021, 14.

19. Michael Ashkenazi, *What We Know about Intelligence: Foundational Xenology* (New York: Springer, 2017).

20. William Stoeger, "Review of Thomas O'Meara, *Vast Universe*," *Theology and Science* 11, no. 1 (2013): 79.

21. The Orthodox theologian Vladimir Lossky notes Orthodox theologies with openings to further civilizations. Jewish writings are not afraid of the idea of multiple worlds; the *Zohar* says that each wise person on Earth is given an inhabited star or planet to lead and direct, and thereby that person advances in the spiritual life. All intelligent creatures have their own image, as individuals and as species (Arnould, *Turbulences*, 219). The Qur'an speaks of Allah's seven heavens and of "the living creatures he has spread forth" (Qur'an 42:30). Hinduism sees a cosmic cycle of hundreds of thousands of years marked by various realizations of creatures; Buddhism expects there to be extraterrestrials (see Arnould, *Turbulences*, 136.). For Chinese traditions on this topic see Ross Andersen, "Closer Encounters: The New Hunt for Extraterrestrials," *The Atlantic*, December 2017, 44–53. David Weintraub deals with religions' view of extraterrestrials at length in *Religions and Extraterrestrial Life: How Will We Deal with It?* (New York: Springer, 2014), 111–204.

22. John F. Haught, "Theology after Contact: Religion and Extraterrestrial Intelligent Life," *Annals of the New York Academy of Sciences* 950 (2001): 301.

23. John F. Haught, *Deeper Than Darwin: The Prospect for Religion in the Age of Evolution* (Boulder, CO: Westview, 2003), 178. "A universe in which intelligent life is an essential rather than accidental discovery could hardly be called purposeless" (Haught, *Science and Faith*, 174).

24. For Origen in the third century, metaphysical and physical separation from the Supreme Intelligence brought about moral corruption, while for the German philosopher Friedrich Schelling in the

nineteenth century there was an inevitable moral fall for intelligences as their existence developed; they fell into limitations in the process by which God sought to become fully realized. For Paul Tillich and not a few modern Protestant theologians, existence essentially involves selfishness, and moral failure is a concomitant of freedom.

25. Seth Shostak, "The Value of L," in *Cosmos and Culture*, ed. S. Dick and M. Lupisella (Washington, DC: NASA, 2009), 412.

26. An extensive treatment of how Christian astrotheologies need not be drawn into scientific or theological pessimism is David Wilkinson, *Christian Eschatology and the Physical Universe* (New York: T&T Clark, 2010). Religion is not mainly about suffering even if it is so for some groups on Earth; see the essays in Ted Peters et al., eds., *The Evolution of Evil* (Göttingen: Vandenhoeck & Ruprecht, 2008).

27. C. S. Lewis, *Out of the Silent Planet* (New York: Macmillan, 1990), 130. Voltaire agreed: "In the hundred thousand millions of worlds dispersed over the regions of space everything goes on by degrees. Our little terraquaeous globe here is the madhouse of those hundred thousand millions of worlds" ("Memnon," in *Favorite Works of Voltaire* [Garden City, NY: De Luxe, 1900], 265).

28. There are other novels depicting worlds not filled with sin. James Blish described the visit of a Jesuit professor to a planet where the people have no acquaintance with evil and live solely by their reason. He cannot convince them to find any meaning in belief, divine revelation, or religion of any kind. The Jesuit wonders whether this kind of Eden is in fact the creation of evil to push aside any possibility of divine inspiration and presence. This brings about a new, strange conflict between faith and reason: *A Case of Conscience* (New York: Random House, 1958).

29. See Arnould, *Turbulences*, 141.

CHAPTER 5

1. Michael Crowe, *The Extraterrestrial Life Debate, Antiquity to 1915: A Source Book* (Notre Dame: University of Notre Dame Press, 2008), 521. For historical information on this topic in theology see Jacques Arnould, *Turbulences dans l'univers: Dieu, les extraterrestres et nous* (Paris: Editions Albin Michel, 2017), and Armin Kreiner,

Jesus, UFOs, Aliens: Außerirdische Intelligenz als Herausforderung für den christlichen Glauben (Freiburg: Herder, 2011).

2. Epicurus cited in Steven Dick, *The Plurality of Worlds: The Origins of the Extraterrestrial Life Debate from Democritus to Kant* (New York: Cambridge University Press, 1984), 17.

3. For Origen, the preexistent intelligence destined to serve as the soul of Jesus born in Bethlehem did not fall. Joined to the Word of God, this intelligence animated the man Jesus, son of Mary and Joseph, through whom the Word taught humanity about its life and destiny. For some views of theologians in the fourth and fifth centuries, see John Chrysostom, *De incomprehensibili Dei natura* 4.2, *Patrologia Graeca* (Migne), vol. 48, 729; Athanasius, *Oratio contra gentes* 39, *Patrologia Graeca* (Migne), vol. 25, 80; Basil, *In Hexameron, Homilia* 3, 3, *Patrologia Greece* (Migne), vol. 29, 57–58; Ambrose, *In Hexahedron* 2.2, *Patrologia Latina* (Migne), vol. 24, 146.

4. Bonaventure, *Commentaria in quatuor libros sententiarum*, lib. 1, dist. 44, art. 1, quaest. 4 (*Opera Omnia* 1, 789) (Quaracchi: Collegium S. Bonaventurae, 1882).

5. See Ignatius Brady, "William of Vaurouillon, O. Min.," *Miscellanea Melchor de Pobladura*, vol. 1 (Rome: Institutum Historicum OFM Cap., 1964), 291–315; Franz Pelster, "Wilhelm von Vorillon, ein Skotist des 15. Jahrhunderts," *Franziskanische Studien* 8 (1921): 48–66; Grant McColley and W. H. Miller, "Saint Bonaventure, Francis Mayron, William Vorilong, and the Doctrine of a Plurality of Worlds," *Speculum* 12 (1937): 388–89; on Bonaventure and the Franciscan school, see Ilia Delio, "Christ and Extraterrestrial Life," *Theology and Science* 5 (2007): 249–65.

6. Guillaume de Vaurouillon, *Quattuor librorum sententiarum compendium venerabilis patris fratris Guillermi Vorrillonis*, lib. 1, dist. xliv (Basel: Langerdorf, 1510), folio 105.

7. Vaurouillon, *Quattuor librorum sententiarum*, folio 105.

8. Vaurouillon, *Quattuor librorum sententiarum*, folio 105.

9. Vaurouillon, *Quattuor librorum sententiarum*, folio 105.

10. See Bruno, *On the Infinite, the Universe, and the Worlds* (1584); a century later, there is Bernard le Bovier de Fontenelle, *Conversations on the Plurality of Worlds* (1686) (Berkeley: University of California Press, 1990).

TOWARD A COSMIC THEOLOGY

11. Thomas Paine, *The Age of Reason* (Secaucus: Citadel Press, 1974), 90. Around 1755, Immanuel Kant wrote in *Universal Natural History and Theory of the Heavens* that there were several planets with inhabitants; they were too wise to sin. At that time, there is William Hay, *Religio philosophi or the Principles of Morality and Christianity Illustrated from a View of the Universe, and of Man's Situation in It* (London: J. Dodsleym, 1771) and Johan Bode, *Anleitung zu Kenntnis des gestirnten Himmels* (Berlin: Himburg, 1792).

12. Alexander Pope, *An Essay on Man* (Princeton, NJ: Princeton University Press, 2016), 8.

13. Ralph Waldo Emerson, "Sermon CLVII," *The Complete Sermons of Ralph Waldo Emerson*, 4, ed. Wesley T. Mott (Columbia: University of Missouri Press, 1989), 159.

14. Emerson, "Sermon CLVII," 159. In 1854, David Brewster published *More Worlds Than One: The Creed of the Philosopher and the Hope of the Christian* (New York: Robert Carter, 1854). In 1890, Ellen White, one of the founders of the Seventh-day Adventist Church, argued that the Word of God, passing "from star to star, from world to world, superintending all," found sin on Earth and became incarnate to save humanity. This is "a mystery which the sinless intelligences of other worlds desired to understand" (Ellen White, *The Story of Patriarchs and Prophets* [1922; repr., Mountain View, CA: Pacific Press, 1948], 69).

15. Ralph Waldo Emerson, "Sermon CLVII," 158. Christianity should set aside the centrality of atonement even as it advocates the moral law and retains some vague role for Jesus as "the gracious instrument of [God's] bounty to instruct men in the character of God and the true nature of spiritual good" ("Sermon CLVII," 159).

16. Domenico Grasso, "La Teologia e la pluralità dei mondi abitati," *La Civiltà Cattolica* 193 (1952): 265. Douglas Vakoch has assembled a survey of Roman Catholic theologies in the recent century ("Roman Catholic Views of Extraterrestrial Intelligence: Anticipating the Future by Examining the Past," in *When SETI Succeeds: The Impact of High-Information Contact*, ed. A. Tough (Bellevue, WA: Foundation for the Future, 2000), 165–74.

17. Karl Rahner, "Sternenbewohner. Theologisch," *Lexikon für Theologie und Kirche* 9 (Freiburg: Herder, 1964), 1061–62; see

Notes

Rahner, "Landung auf dem Mond," *Kritisches Wort: Aktuelle Probleme in Kirche und Welt* (Freiburg: Herder, 1970), 233–34. See Bela Weissmahr, "Die von Karl Rahner herausgestellte Affinität von evolutiver Weltanschauung und christlichem Glauben," *Die philosophischen Quellen der Theologie Karl Rahners*, ed. H. Schöndorf and P. Henrici (Freiburg: Herder, 2005), 175–80; Phillip Geister, *Aufhebung zur Eigentlichkeit: Zur Problematik kosmologischer Eschatologie in der Theologie Karl Rahners* (Uppsala: Uppsala University Press, 1996), 119–21; Denis Edwards, "Resurrection of the Body and Transformation of the Universe in the Theology of Karl Rahner," *Philosophy and Theology* 18 (2006): 357–83.

18. Rahner, "Natural Science and Reasonable Faith," *Theological Investigations* 21 (New York: Crossroad, 1988), 51.

19. Rahner, "Christology within an Evolutionary View," *Theological Investigations* 5 (Baltimore: Helicon, 1966), 173.

20. Rahner, "Christology within an Evolutionary View," 173.

21. Rahner, "Natural Science and Reasonable Faith," *Theological Investigations* 21, 52. Reginaldo Francisco reports a conversation between Jean Guitton and Pope Paul VI in which the pope finds the reality of extraterrestrials reasonable and sees how "the universal church" would include more than Earth ("Possibilità di una redenzione cosmica," in *Origini, l'Universo, la Vita, l'Intelligenza*, ed. F. Bertola et al. [Padua: Il Poligrafo, 1994], 121–40). For similar views from the important theologian Yves Congar see "Has God Peopled the Stars?" in *Wide World My Parish* (Westminster: Newman, 1961); Thomas O'Meara, "Yves Congar: Theologian of Grace in a Wide World," in *Yves Congar: Theologian of the Church*, ed. Gabriel Flynn (Grand Rapids: Eerdmans, 2005), 371–99.

22. Arnould, *Turbulences dans l'univers*, 183.

23. Arnould, *Turbulences dans l'univers*, 247–48.

24. Armin Kreiner, *Jesus, UFOs, Aliens*, 187.

25. Armin Kreiner, *Jesus, UFOs, Aliens*, 202.

26. John F. Haught, "What If ETs Exist?" in *Science and Faith: A New Introduction* (Mahwah, NJ: Paulist Press, 2012), 168. "A universe in which intelligent life is an essential rather than accidental property could hardly be called purposeless," at 175.

27. See John F. Haught, *Resting on the Future: Catholic Theology for an Unfinished Universe* (New York: Bloomsbury, 2015).

28. John F. Haught, *The New Cosmic Story: Inside our Awakening Universe* (New Haven, CT: Yale University Press, 2017), 35; see Kathryn Denning, "Are We Alone? Estimating the Prevalence of Extraterrestrial Intelligence," in *Civilizations beyond Earth: Extraterrestrial Life and Society*, ed. Douglas Vakoch and Albert Harrison (New York: Bergmann Books, 2011), 74–84.

29. Haught, *Science and Faith*, 69.

30. Haught, *Science and Faith*, 169.

CHAPTER 6

1. Aquinas, *Summa Theologiae* (*ST*) III, q. 8, a. 3.

2. See Raymond Brown, *The Gospel According to John I – XII* (Garden City, NY: Doubleday & Company, 1966), 32.

3. Congar, "The Holy Spirit in the Cosmos," in *The Word and the Spirit* (San Francisco: Harper and Row, 1986), 93. The phrase *hypostatic union* in Greek Christian theologies means one coordinating divine person taking on a complete and individualized human nature. The Word sustains metaphysically the man Jesus. Astrotheologies with a wider perspective would have to be wary of the intrusions of contemporary forms of old Christologies poorly understood. Pierre Teilhard de Chardin spoke of the need for a further Council of Nicaea to face the issues of the historical Jesus and the cosmic Christ (see J. A. Lyons, *The Cosmic Christ in Origen and Teilhard de Chardin* [London: Oxford University Press, 1982]).

4. See J. Michl, "Engel IV (Christlich)," in *Reallexikon für Antike und Christentum* (Stuttgart: Anton Hiersemann, 1962), 5:121–23; G. Bareille, "Ange, d'après les Pères," in *Dictionnaire de théologie catholique* 1:1 (Paris: Letouzey et Ané, 1930), 1195–98. In his opening lines on angels, Thomas Aquinas argued firmly against the idea that these powerful and different creatures have any trace of corporeality, although he knew that some early theologians held this view (*ST* I, q. 50, aa. 1 and 2).

5. Lyons, *The Cosmic Christ in Origen and Teilhard de Chardin*, 139.

Notes

6. Aquinas, *Super Evangelium Ioannis Lectura* (1:4) (Turin: Marietti, 1952), ch. 1, lect. 3, 20; on Albert the Great, see Jacques Arnould, *Turbulences en l'univers. Dieu, les extraterrestres et nous*, (Paris: Albin Michel, 2017), 42.

7. Aquinas, *ST* III, q. 16, a. 6 and a. 12; q. 17, a. 2. Thomist scholars in the seventeenth century presented a valuable insight when puzzling over how some traditional Christologies negated a human personality because it had been absorbed by the divine personality in Jesus. They observed that the divine person (personality, hypostasis) would contain, because it is divine, the reality of every possible personality and person seminally, virtually, in an eternal fullness.

8. Arnould, *Turbulences en l'univers*, 39–41.

9. Arnould, *Turbulences en l'univers*, 50–54. In March 1277, the bishop of Paris Tempier condemned a list of errors that he perceived in the areas of philosophy and theology stimulated by the new Aristotelianism. Some of these sought to defend the independence of divine power. One of the issues was God's capability of creating other worlds. Aquinas was skeptical of this because the universe had a unity, focus, and organization. Subsequently, various theologians like Henri of Gent, Richard Middleton, and Jean Buridan (rector of the University of Paris) followed the direction of plurality; see Jean-Pierre Torrell, *The Person and His Work*, Saint Thomas Aquinas, vol. 1 (Washington, DC: Catholic University of America Press, 1996), 298–303; Kent Emery and Andreas Speer, "After the Condemnation of 1277: New Evidence, New Perspectives, and Grounds for New Interpretations," in *Nach der Verurteilung von 1277: Philosophie und Theologie an der Universität von Paris im letzten Viertel des 13. Jahrhunderts*, ed. Jan Aertsen and Kent Emery (Berlin: Walter De Gruyter, 2001), 1–28.

10. Aquinas, *ST* III, q. 31, a. 4. "In a new way God unites himself to a creature, or, rather, unites the creature to himself" (*ST* III, q. 1, a. 1, ad 1).

11. Aquinas, *ST* III, q. 3, a. 7.

12. Giordano Bruno, "Dialogue 4," in *The Ash Wednesday Supper* (The Hague: Mouton, 1975), 134; see Jean-François Robredo, *Les Métamorphoses du ciel. De Giordano Bruno à l'Abbé Lemaître* (Paris:

Presses Universitaires de France, 2018); Steven Dick, ed., *Many Worlds: The New Universe, Extraterrestrial Life & the Theological Implications* (Cambridge: International Society for Science and Religion, 2007), 167–76.

13. Karl Rahner, *Foundations of Christian Faith: An Introduction to the Idea of Christianity* (New York: Crossroad, 1987), 197; see Rahner, "Christology within an Evolutionary View," in *Theological Investigations* 5 (Baltimore: Helicon, 1966), 173.

14. Rahner, *Foundations of Christian Faith*, 196.

15. Karl Rahner, "Natural Science and Reasonable Faith," *Theological Investigations* 21 (New York: Crossroad, 1988), 51.

16. On history in God, see Rahner, *Foundations of Christian Faith*, 138–46; see Edmund Arens, ed., *Zeit Denken. Eschatologie im interdisciplinären Diskurs* (Freiburg: Herder, 2010).

17. Arnould, *Turbulences en l'univers*, 26. Ted Peters argues strongly against incarnations beyond Jesus of Nazareth. "The one incarnation of God in the Jesus of Earth's history will suffice for the entire cosmos" ("Astrobiology and Astrochristology," *Zygon* 51, no. 2 [2016]: 493). How that incarnation could be received by civilizations billions of years before 4 BCE or much later in cultures with quite different technologies, mentalities, and languages is not discussed.

18. See Junius Johnson, "Theological Word and Literary Flesh: Bonaventurian Cosmology and the Cosmic Trilogy of C. S. Lewis," *Literature and Theology* 30 (2016): 426–438. Apparently, Lewis wrote a fourth novel, *The Dark Tower* (published posthumously in 1977); here planetary participants view their being and location on a special screen but in a parallel universe.

19. Alice Ann Meynell, "Christ in the Universe," in *The Poems of Alice Meynell* (London: Hollis and Carter, 1947), 63–64.

CHAPTER 7

1. Aquinas, *Summa Theologiae* (ST) I, q. 65, a. 2, ad 1.

2. Aquinas, *ST* I-II, q. 110, a. 2.

3. As we have seen, Franciscan and Eastern Christian theologies affirm that intelligent and free life calls forth shares in divine life.

Notes

4. Matthias Remenyi, "Hoffnung für den ganzen Kosmos: Überlegungen zur kosmischen Eschatologie," in *Zu den letzten Dingen: Neue Perspektiven der Eschatologie*, ed. Thomas Herkert and Matthias Remenyi (Darmstadt: Wissenschaftliche Buchgesellschaft, 2009), 193.

5. See Brian Greene, *The Fabric of the Cosmos: Space, Time, and the Texture of Reality* (New York: Random House, 2004); Thanu Padmanabhan, *Quantum Themes: The Charms of the Microworld* (London: World Scientific, 2009).

6. Joseph Bracken, *Does God Roll Dice? Divine Providence for a World in the Making* (Collegeville, MN: Liturgical, 2012), 143–44, 182–90; *Reciprocal Causality in an Event-Filled World* (New York: Fortress Academic, 2022), 39. See Marc A. Pugliese, *The One, the Many, and the Trinity: Joseph A. Bracken and the Challenge of Process Metaphysics* (Washington, DC: Catholic University of America, 2011).

7. Caleb Scharf, *The Zoomable Universe* (New York: Farrar, Strauss, and Giroux, 2017), 178.

8. Frank Close, et al., *The Particle Odyssey: A Journey to the Heart of Matter* (Oxford: Oxford University Press, 2002), 7.

9. Heidi Ann Russell, "Quantum Anthropology: Reimagining the Human Person as Body/Spirit," *Theological Studies* 74 (2013): 943. "Embodiment is our actualization in space-time; it is our particle property of being definitively located in a particular place as opposed to all possible places; or means making a choice which inevitably means not choosing other paths or courses of action.... As wave functions the human reality unfolds its infinite potentiality. Embodiment is the finite fact that we cannot live all of our infinite potentiality simultaneously" (Heidi Ann Russell, *Quantum Shift: Theological and Pastoral Implications of Contemporary Developments in Science* [Collegeville, MN: Liturgical Press, 2015], 41).

10. "God's special acts within the windows of opportunity are provided by quantum indeterminacy" (John F. Haught, *The Cosmic Adventure: Science, Religion, and the Quest for Purpose* [New York: Paulist Press, 1984], 227).

11. Russell, *Quantum Shift*, 31; see Russell, "Sin, Grace, Freedom, and Choice," in *Quantum Shift*, 45–55.

CHAPTER 8

1. Moses Maimonides, *A Guide for the Perplexed* (New York: E.P. Dutton, 1186), 1, ch. 73, 1, https://oll.libertyfund.org/title/friedlaender-a-guide-for-the-perplexed.

2. Martin Heidegger, *History of the Concept of Time: Prologomena* (Bloomington: Indiana University Press, 1985), 319–20.

3. George Coyne, *Wayfarers in the Cosmos* (New York: Crossroad, 2002), 154–55.

4. Teilhard de Chardin, *The Prayer of the Universe* (New York: Harper & Row, 1973), 120; see the detailed treatment in John F. Haught, *Resting on the Future: Catholic Theology for an Unfinished Universe* (New York: Bloomsbury, 2015), 11ff.

5. Karl Rahner "Theological Observations on the Concept of Time," *Theological Investigations* 11 (New York: Seabury, 1974), 308.

6. Bernard Sesboüé, *The Resurrection and the Life* (Collegeville, MN: Liturgical Press, 1996), 71. Philosophers and mystics in the Middle Ages sought to express a kind of duration beyond time and yet outside eternity: for this they coined the word *aevum*. *Aevum* is not God's eternity and not a planet's succession of days. *Aevum* sought to express a duration that held aspects of both the eternal and the temporal.

7. See David Wilkinson, *Christian Eschatology and the Physical Universe* (New York: T&T Clark, 2010), 182; Robert John Russell, *Cosmology: From Alpha to Omega* (Minneapolis: Fortress Press, 2008), chapters 8–10; Stephen R. L. Clark, "Deep Time: Does It Matter?," in *The Far-Future Universe: Eschatology from a Cosmic Perspective*, ed. George R. Ellis (Philadelphia: Templeton Foundation Press, 2002).

8. Jacques Arnould, *Turbulences dans l'univers. Dieu, les extraterrestres et nous* (Paris: Albin Michel, 2017), 183; see Alan Penny, "The Lifetimes of Scientific Civilizations and the Genetic Evolution of the Brain," in *Civilizations beyond Earth: Extraterrestrial Life and Society*, ed. Douglas Vakoch and Albert Harrison (New York: Berghahn Books, 2011), 60–73.

9. Roger Haight, *Christianity and Science: Toward a Theology of Nature* (Maryknoll, NY: Orbis, 2007), 163.

10. John F. Haught, *Science and Faith: A New Introduction* (Mahwah, NJ: Paulist Press, 2012), 147.

11. Thomas Aquinas, *ST Supplementum* q. 75, a. 3, c.

12. Peter C. Phan, *Living into Death, Dying into Life: A Christian Theology of Death and Life Eternal* (Hobe Sound, FL: Lectio, 2014), 85–87; see Thomas F. O'Meara, *Life beyond Death* (St. Louis: Catholic Health Association, 2019); Raymond Hausoul, *The New Heaven and New Earth: An Interdisciplinary Comparison between Jürgen Moltmann, Karl Rahner, and Gregory Beale* (Eugene, OR: Wipf and Stock Publishers, 2020).

13. Gregory of Nyssa, *The Great Catechism*, trans. William Moore and Henry Austin Wilson, NPNF V, 2nd series (Grand Rapids, MI: Eerdmans, 1979), 483.

14. Clement of Alexandria, "The Instructor," in *Fathers of the Second Century*, ANF 2 (Peabody, MA: Hendrickson, 1994), 210.

15. John F. Haught, *The Promise of Nature: Ecology and Cosmic Purpose* (Eugene, OR: Wipf and Stock, 2004), 142; see 100–104.

16. Joseph Bracken, *Does God Roll Dice? Divine Providence for a World in the Making* (Collegeville, MN: Liturgical, 2012), 133.

17. Brian Robinette, *Grammars of Resurrection: A Christian Theology of Presence and Absence* (New York: Crossroad, 2009), 153, 164–65.

18. Haught, *Resting on the Future* (New York: Bloomsbury, 2015), 170.

19. Heidi Ann Russell, *Quantum Shift: Theological and Pastoral Implications of Contemporary Developments in Science* (Collegeville, MN: Liturgical Press, 2015), 161.

20. Haught, *Resting on the Future*, 171.

CHAPTER 9

1. Alan Scott, *Origen and the Life of the Stars: A History of an Idea* (Oxford: Clarendon University Press, 1991), 133.

2. See Carl Sagan, *The Varieties of Scientific Experience: A Personal View of the Search for God* (New York: Penguin, 2006), 103.

3. Contrary to Margaret Wertheim, *The Pearly Gates of Cyberspace* (New York: Norton, 1999), intelligent animals living on planets

are not related to angels but to people on Earth. For an extensive discussion of angels, devils, and anthropoid races on Earth, see Jacques Arnould, *Turbulences dans l'univers. Dieu, les extraterrestres et nous* (Paris: Albin Michel, 2017).

4. Serge Brunier, *The Great Atlas of the Stars* (Buffalo, NY: Firefly, 2001), 96–98; see Jean-Pierre Lummet, "Clusters and Super-clusters of Galaxies," in *Cambridge Atlas of Astronomy* (Cambridge: Cambridge University, 1994), 399. "Voids are surrounded by relatively thick layers into which nearly all galaxies are crowded." See "Voids," in *Dictionary of Geophysics, Astrophysics, and Astronomy*, ed. Richard A. Matzner (Boca Raton: CRC Press, 2001), 505.

5. See Dominique Lestel, "Ethology, Ethnology, and Communication with Extraterrestrial Intelligence," Douglas Vakoch, ed., *Archaeology, Anthropology, and Interstellar Communication* (Washington, DC: NASA, 2014) 227–28.

6. See Douglas Vakoch, *On Orbit and Beyond: Psychological Perspectives on Human Spaceflight* (New York: Springer, 2013); *Psychology of Space Exploration: Contemporary Research in Historical Perspective* (Washington, DC: NASA, 2011); and Stephen Webb, *If the Universe Is Teeming with Aliens...Where Is Everybody? Fifty Solutions to the Fermi Paradox and the Problem of Extraterrestrial Life* (New York: Praxis, 2002).

7. Jill Tarter, "Exoplanets, Extremophiles, and the Search for Extraterrestrial Intelligence," in *Communication with Extraterrestrial Intelligence,* ed. Douglas Vakoch (Albany: State University of New York Press, 2011), 3–18; this volume contains a further thirty-two essays on communications with extraterrestrials.

8. Douglas Vakoch, "Reconstructing Distant Civilizations and Encountering Alien Cultures," in *Archaeology, Anthropology, and Interstellar Communication*, ed. Douglas Vakoch (Washington, DC: NASA, 2014), xiv.

9. Douglas Vakoch, "Reconstructing Distant Civilizations and Encountering Alien Cultures," xiv; for the history of searches prior to SETI see A. Harrison and D. Vakoch, "The Search for Extraterrestrial Intelligence as an Interdisciplinary Effort," in *Civilizations beyond Earth: Extraterrestrial Life and Society* (New York: Bergbahn Books, 2011), 1–30.

10. Michio Kaku, *Physics of the Future* (New York: Random House, 2012), 396: see Cooper, "2lst Century SETI," in *The Contact Paradox: Challenging Our Assumptions in the Search for Extraterrestrial Intelligence* (New York: Bloomsbury Sigma, 2019).

11. On science fiction and movies see Don Lincoln, *Alien Universe: Extraterrestrial Life in Our Minds and in the Cosmos* (Baltimore: The Johns Hopkins University Press, 2013); David Siegel Bernstein, "Reading/Movie/Song List," in *Blockbuster Science: The Real Science in Science Fiction* (Amherst, NY: Prometheus Books, 2017).

12. See Ted Peters, et al., *The Evolution of Evil* (Gottingen: Vandenhoeck & Rurprecht, 2008).

13. John F. Haught, *Resting on the Future: Catholic Theology for an Unfinished Universe* (New York: Bloomsbury, 2015), 120–26.

CHAPTER 10

1. Nancy Ellen Abrams and Joel Primack, *The New Universe and the Human Future* (New Haven, CT: Yale University Press, 2011), 6.

2. Abrams and Primack, *The New Universe and the Human Future*, 153.

3. See Carl Sagan, *Carl Sagan's Cosmic Connection*, produced by Jerome Agel (Cambridge: Cambridge University Press, 2000), 257–58.; Jan Narveson, "Martians and Morals: How to Treat an Alien," in *Extraterrestrials: Science and Alien Intelligence*, ed. Edward Regis (Cambridge: Cambridge University Press, 1985), 245–66.

4. John F. Haught, *Deeper than Darwin* (Boulder, CO: Westview Press, 2003), 179; see Stephen R. L. Clark, "Deep Time: Does It Matter?," in *The Far-Future Universe: Eschatology from a Cosmic Perspective*, ed. George R. Ellis (Philadelphia: Templeton Foundation Press, 2002).

5. See Heidi Ann Russell, "Quantum Anthropology. Reimagining the Human Person as Body/Spirit," *Theological Studies* 74 (2013): 959.

6. James Gardner, "The Intelligent Universe," in *Cosmos and Culture: Cultural Evolution in a Cosmic Context*, ed. Steven J. Dick and M. Lupisella (Washington, DC: NASA, 2009), 379.

7. Lupisella, "Cosmocultural Evolution," in *Cosmos and Culture*, 324.

8. The sermon "Beati qui habitant" in T. Kaeppeli, "Una raccolta di prediche attribuite a S. Tommaso d'Aquino," *Archivum Fratrum Praedicatorum* 13 (1943): 88–89.

9. Aquinas, *Summa Theologiae (ST) Supplementum*, q. 84, a. 1. In the eschaton do these glorified humans pass from one place to another in an instant, or do they pass through some kind of interval as they change their location? Such questions were of great interest in Aquinas's time, and he considers them here.

10. Aquinas, *ST Supplementum*, q. 84, a. 2.

11. Guy Consolmagno, "The Consolation of Constellations," *The Tablet* 274 (2020): 30; see Paul Schutz, "Cultivating a 'Cosmic Perspective' in Theology: Reading William R. Stoeger with *Laudato Si*," *Theological Studies* 80 (2019): 798–821.

12. Thomas Berry, *The Christian Future and the Fate of Earth* (Maryknoll, NY: Orbis, 2009), 115, 117; see Vitor Westhelle, *Eschatology and Space* (New York: Palgrave Macmillan, 2012), 1–15.

13. Christian de Duve concludes, "Priests are still needed, as are thinkers, scientists, philosophers, poets, writers, musicians, sculptors, painters and other artists....We need priests—or better said, *spiritual guides* for this, avoiding the pomp of robes and rites that surrounds the historical image of the priest—to serve as mentors who, without dogmatism or fundamentalism, can inspire, help, and orient." Christian de Duve, *Life Evolving: Molecules, Mind, and Meaning* (Oxford: Oxford University Press, 2002), 306.

14. See Victor Hayes, *What Are They Saying about the End of the World?* (New York: Paulist Press, 1983), 23–27.

15. Peter C. Phan, *Responses to 101 Questions on Death and Eternal Life* (New York: Paulist Press, 1997), 108; see *Eternity in Time: A Study of Karl Rahner's Eschatology* (Cranberry, NJ: Associated University Presses, 1988).

16. John F. Haught, *Resting on the Future: Catholic Theology for an Unfinished Universe* (New York: Bloomsbury, 2015), 126, 146–47.

17. John F. Haught, *Christianity and Science: Toward a Theology of Nature* (Maryknoll, NY: Orbis, 2007), 63.